The Poeming Pigeon
A Literary Journal of Poetry

The Poeming Pigeon
A Literary Journal of Poetry

Volume 3, Issue 1
Poems from the Garden

A Publication of The Poetry Box®

©2017 The Poetry Box®
All rights reserved.
Each poem copyright reserved by individual authors.
Original Cover Illustration & Photographs by Robert R. Sanders.
Editing & Book Design by Shawn Aveningo Sanders.
Cover Design by Robert R. Sanders.
Printed in the United States of America.

No part of this book may be reproduced
in any matter whatsoever without written
permission from the author, except in the case
of brief quotations embodied in critical essays,
reviews and articles.

Library of Congress Control Number: 2016953120

ISBN-13: 978-0-9980999-0-3
ISBN-10: 0-9980999-0-2

Published by The Poetry Box®, 2017
Beaverton, Oregon
www.ThePoetryBox.com
530.409.0721

With gratitude for honey bees
and those who are fighting to protect them

Contents

Introduction 11
Fertilized by Mark Strand ~*Ada Jill Schneider* 15
Notes from the Underground ~*Eric le Fatte* 16
Oh Worm! ~*Barbara A. Meier* 17
Garden ~*Neil Creighton* 19
Substrate ~*Paul Yager* 20
Compost ~*Heather Angier* 21
Recycling a Well-Tended Garden ~*Tricia Knoll* 23
Planting in March ~*Suzy Harris* 24
Worth Repeating ~*C. Hunter Davis* 25
Heliotrope ~*Alwyn Marriage* 26
Planting Beans by the Moon on a Small City Balcony ~*Allison Thorpe* 27
The Garden ~*G. Murray Thomas* 29
Moby Zucchini ~*Daniel Williams* 30
It's Been a Good Summer ~*Terri Niccum* 32
Harvesting Tomatoes ~*Kelila A Knight* 33
For Kathebela in September ~*Susan Rogers* 35
The Gardeners ~*James B. Nicola* 37
The Better Homes and Gardens New Garden Book — unused ~*Katy Brown* 38
I will not survive the collapse of civilization. ~*Matt Farr* 39
Out Back ~*W.P. Osborn* 40
I Am a Ladybug When ~*Rachelle M. Parker* 42
Cow Parsnip ~*Susan Whitney* 43
The Electricity of Bees ~*Sara Wilson* 44
Catching Daylight ~*Georgette Howington* 45
At Last ~*John Davis* 46
A Gardener's Winter Dream ~*Larry Schug* 47
Renewal ~*Catherine McGuire* 48
Gardening Goddess ~*Jennifer Lagier* 49
A Good Start ~*Emily Pittman Newberry* 50

Bending to Work in the Heat ~*Judith Skillman* 52
The Solitary Gardener ~*Robert Eastwood* 54
On Mowing the Lawn ~*Gareth Culshaw* 56
Sunshine State Serpent Eating Its Tail ~*Karla Linn Merrifield* 57
Calculation ~*Lanette Cadle* 59
Learning Beauty: An Apology to Conifers ~*Suzanne Sigafoos* 60
Death of a Chinese Scholar, or Why I Had to Cut My Twelve-Year-Old
    Japonica Down ~*Carolyn Martin* 61
Maple Seed Pod ~*Lillo Way* 63
the peace the trees give ~*Linda M. Crate* 64
Dreaming the Delirium of Spring ~*Rosemary Douglas Lombard* 65
Waking Vision ~*Carter McKenzie* 67
Chamomile for the Molokans ~*Katy Brown* 68
Unnamed Ghost ~*Cindy Rinne* 69
Forms of Grief ~*Diane Averill* 70
Ice Plant ~*Elizabeth Stoessl* 73
While Deadheading Lavender, I Think of My Late Father ~*Amy Miller* 74
Tending the Garden ~*Kate Wells* 75
In the Garden ~*Margaret Chula* 76
Elegy for Emma ~*Kay Morgan* 77
Roots ~*Marilyn Johnston* 78
Flowers Themselves ~*Beth Suter* 79
Van Gogh Dreams of Iris ~*Ann Howells* 80
Gardens of Light ~*Jeannie E. Roberts* 81
A Walk to the Other Side ~*Stephen Linsteadt* 82
L. tigrinum ~*Phyllis Wax* 83
Aubade with Flowers ~*Stan Zumbiel* 84
A Beautiful Rain ~*Claudine Nash* 85
Tone Painting ~*Liz Nakazawa* 87
Flamenco Dancer ~*Cheryl A. Van Beek* 88
All Wild ~*Ruth Hill* 89
Lawn Party ~*Pamela Ahlen* 90

Writing Poetry Is Not Like Gardening ~*Johanna Ely* 91
Spring Tease ~*Pattie Palmer-Baker*. 92
From the Library of Mussels ~*Dianne Avey* 93
Magnolia, After a Storm ~*Janet M. Powers*. 94
Tassajara's Roses ~*Tricia Knoll*. 95
Notes from an August Gardener ~*Carolyn Martin* 97
The End of the Season ~*Marilyn Johnston* 99
For Their Own Good ~*Brad G. Garber* 100
Blight ~*Alec Solomita* 101
Garden in Amherst ~*Laurinda Lind* 102
Lilith ~*Brittney Corrigan* 103
Queens Kitchen ~*Brigit Truex* 105
Dynasty Dandelion ~*Tim Kahl* 106
Ecliptical Allegory ~*Scott A. Russell* 107
Once in a Blue Moon ~*Irene Bloom* 108
The Indictment of Flowers ~*Sherry Wellborn*. 109
Fargugium with Exclamation Point ~*Kenneth Pobo*. 110
After Election Day ~*Michael Baldwin*. 111
The Remembrance Poppy ~*M. Wright* 112
If We Hadn't Lost Eden ~*Steve Williams*. 113
In This Garden ~*Laurie Kolp*. 115
Today, I Will Only Attend to the Small Things ~*Viola Weinberg*. 116
Gently on My Mind ~*Shari Jo LeKane-Yentumi* 117
Blaze ~*Annie Lighthart*. 118
Therefore Eternal ~*Cathy Cain*. 119
And on Earth, the Garden of the Universe ~*Linda Ferguson*. 120
Acknowledgments 123
Contributors 125
Index of Poets (by last name) 137
About The Poetry Box® 141
Order Form 143

Introduction

True confession time. I am not much of a gardener. I have what you might call a *brown* thumb. I have a habit of overwatering or under-watering, as well as placing flowers based on where *I want them to grow* rather than where they *can grow*. I have foolishly planted impatiens and pansies in the full afternoon sun and have tried to forcibly brighten the shadiest corner of the yard with sun-loving plants like marigolds.

But oh, how I admire a beautiful bounty of flowers and gardens that seem to effortlessly bloom year round with an assortment of perennials and annuals — each plant bringing a beautiful new surprise. In fact, one of the best things about moving to Portland in the dead of winter, was that first year of discovery in our own backyard.

Daffodils, jonquils, crocus and tulips popped up to greet us in the early spring. The rhododendrons had their own schedule of blooming — first the pale pink bush out back, then the lavender bush in the corner and then bright rosy pink closing out the show. There's a hydrangea with the most unique teal blue clusters I've ever seen; it has a rose bush hiding in the middle, whose branches snake up to my desk window to greet me with hot pink beauties that are simply breathtaking. We've enjoyed snacking on cherries as we dodged the dive-bombing blue jays. And then there was the trellis covered in a vine that I originally thought might be wisteria. Surprise! We've got grapes! And what fun we had sharing the gift with the robins, who seemed to wobble a bit after indulging on the overripe fruit that was beginning to ferment on the vine.

Yes, gardens bring joy! And who doesn't need a little more joy these days? I think Suzy Harris said it best in her poem "Planting in March"

> *We need this — to get dirt under our fingernails,*
> *scatter seeds in the freshly dug soil*
> *and then be astonished by what survives.*

It's obvious that gardens can heal and help us cope with difficult life (and death) struggles, as this was certainly one of the recurring themes discovered reading through the stacks of submitted poems. A multitude of cultures use flowers to mark the start or end of life, and the passing through to perhaps a new realm, whether it be congratulatory flowers sent to a new mother, graduate or bride, or the splay of gladiolas and white lilies at a memorial. But it goes beyond that. On these pages you'll read heartbreaking stories of still-born children buried under the Sakura trees at an internment camp, tales of forgiveness and remembrance, and a walled garden built to not only honor those lost, but as a way to deal with a lifetime of grief in Diane Averill's gorgeous poem, "Forms of Grief"

> *… One of my soul-sisters,*
> *Pam, died of cancer. Too soon! Molly and I cried.*
> *We were three, so I plant a trillium for us.*

Of course there's more to gardening than pretty petals and posies. We've got poems about growing and sharing vegetables. What a glorious way to build community and communion. My husband has a much greener thumb than me, so when he decided to plant tomatoes in our backyard, I wasn't really ready for the abundance of fruit, nor the overwhelming joy I felt sampling our first harvest. Nothing — and I mean nothing — is as delicious as biting into a just-plucked tomato still warm from the sun. The next year we added peppers and zucchini, giving me a chance to tryout my grandmother's prize-winning zucchini bread recipe. So when I read Daniel Williams, "Moby Zucchini," I couldn't help but smile. I'll let you discover the delightful ending that started out as:

> *a botanical monster that began life*
> *as a lovely golden blossom nurtured*
> *beneath palmate leaves of its mother*

No one ever said gardening was easy work. It takes tenacity, patience and a strong back. And it helps if you don't have allergies. The gardener can't be squeamish about worms, spiders or natural fertilizer. For the dedicated gardener, composting becomes a way of life, for they know a good garden starts from the ground up. Proper prepping of the soil in the 'off season' brings great rewards, and many have their own secret rituals when planting season arrives. Allison Thorpe heeds her grandmother's advice in "Planting Beans by the Moon on a Small City Balcony"

> *bless the seeds and pat them to bed*
> *like you would tired children,*
>
> *turn three times against the wind,*
> *then jig as the calling hits you.*

Whether you feel the call for dirt under your fingernails and doing a jig under the moon, or enjoy pruning roses at a community garden, or simply need a break from the world's headlines to get back to nature and tend to the beautiful small things in life, we hope you enjoy reading these poems from the garden. And if the weeds take over the yard and caterpillars attack your heirlooms, may the poetry blooming from these pages make you smile.

~ Shawn Aveningo Sanders
April, 2017

Ada Jill Schneider

Fertilized by Mark Strand
"I have been eating poetry."

Sun sweat drips into my eyes,
sonnets bounce in the rain;
in a garden patch mulched with feelings
I have been planting poetry.

The earth is mealy, rich with fragrant
lavender, scented geraniums. I tousle each
flower, *mot juste*; prune, lop and top
till my face is red as rhubarb.

I want to spray cool water over my head
till puddles form in my yellow *Jollys*,
trickle into rivulets circling pale sage,
licorice tarragon, lickable, palpable

poetry I cultivate. My roots dig deep
into time, reaching Rachel's tomb.
Lush psalms spill out of my basket
and I swear I attract hummingbirds.

Notes from the Underground

Fish, one foot
under, buried
beneath each plant,
fins set on red
alert: a trick
from Tisquantum
via pilgrims
swims down
to us. Tropicals
among foxgloves,
mackerels with composites,
Mister Lincoln's rose
over the great white shark:
these are the schools
that make stuff grow.

Never content,
an avid gardener
inspects less
than perfect blooms,
and leans over
the pink tulip
as if to call orders
through a megaphone
to the deep:
Get to work
down there!
They roll
subservient eyes
and fertilize.

Barbara A. Meier

Oh Worm!

Oh Worm,
residing in dirt,
chewing life in a toothless mouth,
excreting pellet remains:
Death Wreaths.

Your trace,
compacts into tunnels,
surface to bedrock.
No eyes to see
no ears to hear
just vibrations of terror-
the mole victorious!

Oh Worm!
death surrounds you,
above,
below,
your suicide on cement,
your protracted body,
noose-like in death,
a sodden spasm.
The silence in thunder
and the whimper of lightning.

O Death, you worm,
you litter my path.
I dodge your corpses,
I tip toe around your limp remains.
Ignore the fossil prints,
etched on cement.
You are everywhere I look.
You are the worm in gall,

the absinthe:
green death in carpets above.

The wormwood of dirt,
pattering the bronze,
dimming the lights,
making passages through bone.

Oh Worm!
Compost my body!
Make soil of my remains!
My breath, fleet feet,
you cannot catch,
coalesces in the heavens!

For all I am is dirt on earth
and breath in heaven above.

The rain that drives
to drown
lays on amalgamated
surface,
the leachate formed by body and water,
rebirthing.

Oh Worm! Oh Death!
Fear not thy grave!

Neil Creighton

Garden

I scratch beneath the skin of ground.
feel a heart in rhythmic beat,
vastness, strength and pulsing life
in the soil beneath my feet.

I see an exhalation of breath
scud clouds and sway leaves,
form ponds, rivers and lakes
from deep communion with the seas.

A wind song is in my heart,
a slant of light inside my brain.
I know scents more rich than wine.
I absorb steady soft soak of rain.

Yes, it holds me in its arms.
I hear its blended notes rejoice.
To songs of cricket, bird and breeze
I add my own still small voice.

It sustains me, gives me life,
richly enfolds me all around.
See, it will hold me in its arms
even when I lie in the ground.

Substrate

And dirt now gets its turn,
from lowest, meanest element
it now becomes substrate and anchor bed —
soil, fertile earth,
life-giver to all terrestrial life.

Not dirt as filth, repugnant,
but womb that nurtures all new growth —
grave that cradles all remains,
origin and end
to every living thing.

Compost

The camellias are selling it;
each lusty bloom —
a gorgeous heart
throbbing—*love, oh love*

think of it:

wrapped in quiet
moonlight — I trace
your graying sideburns,
the crow's feet stamped
across your face — and listen
to our old, sold hearts
thumping.

Well, what, so what
that flowers fade, drop
one by one, some-
times in pairs,
to the garden below.

This is love, they yell
falling, *love*

think of it:

all those open hearts
on open hearts — heaps
and heaps of them —
eventually raked, shoveled
into bruised, soggy piles

and look at us
all the while
vaguely aware
something lovely
can still grow from it.

Tricia Knoll

Recycling a Well-Tended Garden

She side-bends and stoops
after decades of puttering limber-up
work-in-dirt yoga, knee bends to growing graces.

Her garden sprawls on its back,
open palms to June sun, humming
a hover and rest like the blue darner.

Her fingers spread compost,
sifting the strumming
of vegetable patches into mantras —
mantras learned in years of garden work —

Welcome guests —
flyers, buzzers, diggers, peckers, chewers.

Love is green. Nothing clashes with it.

Every worm is worth rescuing.

Wisdom does not come easily; dirty fingernails do.

Weeds ask how we got here.

Sing without fear. Soil knows eccentricity.

Wiggle in womb water.

Seed packets recycle
like wishes.

Though minds wander
from memory to future sight,
gardens stay put.

Planting in March

My love, I have brought you seeds:
three kinds of peas, arugula and radishes.
We can plant now, while we feel hopeful.

Digging in the dirt is a kind of dance, too.
Shovel in, shovel out, mixing in compost
to lighten the clay earth, like yeast for bread.

We need this — to get dirt under our fingernails,
scatter seeds in the freshly dug soil
and then be astonished by what survives.

C. Hunter Davis

Worth Repeating

Above the sandstone the sun again puts back
the sherbet it stole at dawn
The pinion jay acrobats in yet another flight
across the peaks, swooping down to
refresh, knowing that tomorrow he will make
trip after trip. He nestles in, looking forward to the
repeating in the day ahead.

The cottonwood smells the night,
contributing her comfort scent to the mix.
Once more stretching roots to the stream.
Morning she will find the breeze for leaves to sway
back and forth back and forth.

The sego lily catches dew by
opening and closing,
reproducing yet another bud for the collared lizard
as it did yesterday and the day before and the day before.

I too put my shoes near the door for the coming walk
up and down up and down the rows
of dahlias and poppies beginning and
ending their growing season.
Up and down I'll go, up and down
swaying in the routine.

Heliotrope

It was the size of a little fingernail
when I dropped it down the hole.
Now wind, rain, snow, hail, light and dark
take turns to form your winter counterpane.

What is happening down below? Tell me, tiny one,
do you suffer claustrophobia, hypothermia
or deathly chill; are you laughing, snug and cosy,
or somersaulting, flirting with the worms?

Are you wide awake and waiting,
or sleeping until you feel the touch of spring?
What troubles you? Is it wet or dry rot, slime
of moluscs or the teeth of rodents?

And is it a struggle or an accident,
when your first green blade begins
to break the earth? Do you, like us,
sometimes fear death and destruction,

or all along hold firm to the belief
that soon you'll stretch towards the sky,
then daily turn your yellow head
to face the sun?

Planting Beans by the Moon on a Small City Balcony

I'm no Juliet, that's for sure,
though the moon winks like a fat Romeo,

and this tenth floor stage
offers no earthy base beneath my feet.

Long from the hills I've traveled,
my fingers ache the dark crumble of soil,

that geography of blue jay and hoot owl,
of garden bright and fragrant.

This wide tray gorged with packaged dirt
will have to do for now.

Bean seeds nestle my palm
like warm bird eggs.

I can hear my grandmother:
poke one finger in the soil knuckle deep,

bless the seeds and pat them to bed
like you would tired children,

turn three times against the wind,
then jig as the calling hits you.

Her mountain superstitions ringing
in my ear, I sow my crop,

spin for my waxing Romeo,
hope my neighbors aren't watching

this mad country woman
jigging her love story to the night,

then I wait for the earth to speak
that voice of green faith rising.

G. Murray Thomas

The Garden

As I pluck your weeds
   I feel the ragged underbrush
   of my mind clearing.
In quiet contemplation
   I pull out
   every errant root
   every errant thought,
Leaving room
   for the important strands
   to bloom.

Every morning —
   fuller leaves
   new crisp life
   hints of flowers and fruit.
And something new
   growing within as well.

My spirit blooms
   with your every flower.
You have nourished me
   long before I taste
   your first salad.

Daniel Williams

Moby Zucchini

Sometimes gardens grow surprises
gardeners know nothing about —
picking cherry tomatoes
you come across an immensity
that has eluded you   discover
a botanical monster that began life
as a lovely golden blossom nurtured
beneath palmate leaves of its mother
a plant that has gone unpicked simply
because no one knew of its existence

I'd reached for a particularly luscious
tomato the color of a ruby when my
hand nudged something solid
a volunteer squash plant
Shoving aside its leaves
I found a huge squash attached
a foot long weighing a pound or so
oddly it was white with some green
and yellow splotches slicing through
its umbilicus I hefted it up

What does one do with a pound of pith?
I'd been eating zucchini all summer
and into September
I was of a mind to relegate it to compost
when I was surprised to see
a pair of dark eyes watching me
over the top rail of my fence the squash
gladly given to weathered tan hands was
just as gladly received by them
to what purpose I did not care

A week later I left home on an errand
upon my return I was surprised to find
a package carefully wrapped in waxed paper
placed in a basket on my doorstep
Everything has value though we may not see it
through the transformative power of kindness
this great white zucchini had become two
golden loaves redolent of nutmeg and allspice
resting still warm from the oven at my front door

It's Been A Good Summer

It's been a good summer for tomatoes
As if the raw earth
Took pity on these foolish humans
Who looked to skyscrapers to save them
Inside and out

Come down, come down,
Says the brown scruff.
Put your ear right here,
No, plant your whole body flat.
Let your hands, your knees carry
A bit of me away. It takes a little time, yes,
But see, if you bow down to me,
I'll give you something back.

Witness these globes mirroring your deepest want:
Alluring red, shining hope
The heart of expectation.
Everyone wants them, most
Anyone can have them if they're willing
To race the fat green worms
To claim them. And face it!
You've done worse.

Open wide!
Soon you will have the sweet
Pang of life
Dripping down your chin

Kelila A Knight

Harvesting Tomatoes

    In her vegetable garden,
        Mom silently plucked
            tomato from vine,

                gently pressed fingers into skin
as if the fruit was her young,
        feverish child and she was
            dabbing cloth against forehead.

            She dropped fruit in red bowl,
told me *This is knowing*
        what it means to be blessed,
            plucked another, felt

                weight in her hand, was satisfied.
Straightening her back
        as much as she could,
            her shoulders were ever-bowed,

                sweat-marked. Feverish, she admitted
fatigue. I begged her to drink
        water and rest —
            I could finish on my own.

                I've done this all my life, she said,
refusing concession.
        With both hands, I plucked
            faster, discarded a mushed tomato.

                        Garden worms had burrowed, marking
Flesh. In vain attempts to claim
            the fruit for themselves,
                            they had speckled the core

with their fingerprints, as if to say
            We too know what it means to be blessed.

Susan Rogers

For Kathabela in September

You are already here
for you are more
than a name
that tells of you

present or not
in the gardens
that you wander
you are every season

every fluttering
petal on flower
or signature hat,
butterfly wing

and sailing leaves
of dancing trees.
Warm wind
and chill of coming fall

no matter to the glint
in your searching eye
seeing shadows
on the ground

and shadows in the air
alike with wonder.
You who have arrived
in this cherished garden

to harvest tomato
and pepper
gather colors in your arms

fire engine red,

shimmering gold
so you can write them
into fragrant verse.
They all know

you have come
to honor them —
share their juice
with eager poets.

You who fly
down garden rows
looking for
invited guests

bow to all
and to the lucky ones,
whisper,
thank you,

as you take them
from the vine
perfect in the sunlight
of your hand.

James B. Nicola

The Gardeners

My neighbor will not only sow
his seeds but post at every row
the emptied pack of seeds to show
what he hopes to grow so
that visitors who come and go
and might be curious can know
what lies, or is supposed to lie, below.

I throw my emptied packs away
and when a neighbor asks what fla-
vor I would be planting today
I smile and wink and do not say.

The Better Homes and Gardens New Garden Book — unused

I'd write about a garden if I could,
a jeweled treasure. But, alas! I'm not
a woman who has ever understood
the charm of tulips striving to arise
from the brutal grasp of hopeless, barren plots.
I can't relate to gardeners' greeny highs,
the raptured praise of growing plants from seed
or tending shoots to fine maturity.

With garden-tools, the poet's hands will bleed.
I can't find the charm in any part
of beds that give no certain surety
that they won't break the gardener's longing heart.
I'd write about a garden — if I could —
in raptured praise of growing life from seed.

Matt Farr

I will not survive the collapse of civilization.

The weeds we pulled made me sneeze.
I wiped my nose with dirt fingernails.
Mud in my mustache tastes like metal.
My knees hurt. My back hurts. I forgot sunscreen.
What's wrong with grocery store tomatoes?

W.P. Osborn

Out Back

It rained
I dug
She mixed
She sowed

Sun shone
Peas grew
Deer showed
They lunched

I stewed
They munched
She waved
They went

She dug
I sowed
They feasted
I raved

She clapped
They bolted
We shopped
We fenced

I dug
She sowed
It warmed
Bugs larvaed

We nipped
We trapped
We screened
We tented

It rained
I dug
She sowed
Corn tasseled

Coons carved
Ears fell
Elms blew
We starved

Rachelle M. Parker

I Am a Ladybug When

I fly, hard, red shell black dotted.
I hunt for other bugs, smaller than me,
ones that I can gobble in one bite.

I know I shouldn't but I get queasy
when first I have to kill them then eat.

I look at my reflection and wonder
if being pretty is all it cracks up to be.

Tricking unsuspecting souls,
luring them into my hungry mouth.

Maybe I can stop eating meat
It could be freeing. Living off vegetation
not consuming another being.

Susan Whitney

Cow Parsnip
(Heracleum maximum)

What cows?
Asked the elk

Contemplating the tender green
the fat ribbed pod

It swelled
Day after day

And cracked open
An umbrella against the sun

White bouquet
Prairie nosegay

Then came the bees

Sara Wilson

The Electricity of Bees

All the bees are electric.
They brush, furred, through the invisible
drizzle and constant deluge of drafts'
shifting charges. It clings to them like pollen,

like rain; and watch them on the threshold of hives
dance to discharge the excess
electrons collected by flight.

Examine the sparkling garden. Every flower
visited is sprinkled with brief lightening,
the graffiti of bees, the little
jolts and novas unloaded with each landing.
Trace shocked flowers like stepping stones
like constellations
between the dull and dark and desired.

Note the static
night sky, all the wayward
bees charged into stars.

Georgette Howington

Catching Daylight

Sunset at 8:30 in late July
the bees go home by 8:00
and there I am hurrying in
the garden with what's left
of the day pressing against
my face as the transparent
undulation of twilight ripples
a faint overcast softening
the once sharp edges of
yellow sunshine changing
the crisp squinting hot day
into a pale cool silver light
filtering through my fingers,
shadows plunging space
as I reach to pluck a red
tomato hidden by the deep
green leaves, and I kneel
listening to crickets begin
their night song while I am
catching daylight just before
the evening takes it away.

John Davis

At Last

        Smelling of sage and wintermint,
Silence walked out of the forest.
        She brushed off the cotton grass
that lined her shoulders
        then folded herself around us
like a quilt of maidenhair ferns
        and warmed what hadn't been warmed
in months of city living.

        Silence held us until leaves grew
from our fingers, leathery leaves
        thick and strongly veined.
We became serrated in the dawn
        with hairy runners and rootstocks.
At last we blossomed and waited,
        the way Silence waited in the sun.
Then we ripened into red strawberries.

Larry Schug

A Gardener's Winter Dream

This food I serve you,
home-grown harvest, gift of sun and rain and soil,
began with a winter dream
dreamed as snow fell outside my window
and I dozed in my rocker beside the fireplace,
seed catalog, open on my lap;
my list of seeds, each a dream itself —
carrots, broccoli, spinach, zucchini,
fallen to the floor beneath my chair.

In this winter dream
I see a garden of straight rows,
plots of potatoes, a jungle of tomatoes.
I dream of myself kneeling as if in prayer,
dirt under my fingernails, sun warm on my back,
a gentle breeze whispering in the trees
as I tend peas and beans, peppers, red and green.
Bumblebees buzz orange and yellow marigolds.
A hummingbird hums in my ear.

I dream of my kitchen,
messy with the work of preservation,
stems and peelings strewn about,
cutting board puddled with juice
the smell of tomatoes stewing in their own sauces,
broccoli steaming like a lover's breath.
And I dream of a table surrounded by family and guests,
the clinking of silverware on earthen plates,
the satisfied silence of people eating their fill.

Catherine McGuire

Renewal

If it weren't for the mushrooms rising
from leaf mold, fungal parishioners

in late winter's church, if it weren't
for gaudy scarlet rhubarb bulges,

vegetable phallus in decaying straw,
I would draw winter around me

like life's last cloak, hunker
in dark rooms, give in to the decay.

But jays scold, flash their sapphire
in bare cherries; improbable shoots push aside

the debris of dead years and shine green
in thin sun, in sky like an enameled

blue-spatter coffeepot. The cycle is not yet done,
may never be. I slip off my shoes,

let my bare feet chill in icy grass
shocking me to life.

Gardening Goddess

Morning glories unfold
when she sings at dawn.
By afternoon, tomatoes swell;
the first apples redden.

Sunset tucks her beneath
silver artichoke arms,
the flowering cape
of a strawberry bed.

All night she dreams of
zucchini and eggplant,
strokes warm dirt like
a quilt's satin binding.

She smiles,
sighs in her sleep.
Secretive carrots stretch.
Juicy radishes fatten.

In the selective stockpile
of post-harvest leavings,
she composts grey ghosts,
what first frost has weeded.

A Good Start

You made me work, like a chain gang,
stuck between deep grass roots
and fast approaching rain,
and my fear of missing
the early growing season.

You made me work,
and I hated it
for the pain in my left foot
where tired parts pound
too hard on flat feet,
for old back muscles,
for a mind's ambitions;

and plans turn to dust
even as I slog
through the mud.

You made me work,
so I smile
at my pretentions
running up against your deep
gnarly grass roots; clearly
you know this ground,
intimately.

You made me work,
and I will return
tomorrow and tomorrow,
for I have foresight
and stubborn genes

on my side,
drawn ever forward
by the thought of tasting
the children
of my sweat.

Bending to Work in the Heat

                Rows and columns,
the corn raising its silk tassels
        in august ceremony,
my mother tethered to her shovel,
breaking red Maryland clay
        into chunks.

Nothing single in that garden —
flies and their cousins,
        the horseflies.
Bees and their sisters,
        the wasps.

The sun spawned
              a twin
    in milk-blue sky.
I remember what needed to be tended —
dirt, virgin zucchini, and tomatoes.

            In pure solicitous warmth
the heat became our primer.
We absorbed its thirsts and irritations,
its longings. I stepped on a hornet.
My gloveless hands found worms
        halved by mother's shovel.

Maternal garden, garden
where Adam and Eve
        melted into one another,
their arms and legs tangled,
        vined like the morning glory.
Whatever the heat wanted it took.

The sun fell into the Potomac by degrees.
A moon rose, cold to the touch —
        pink quartz, exotic dessert.

The Solitary Gardener

Soiled knots, his dirty knuckles,
his face runnelled & leathered.
Call me Smitty, he said, & offered

four bucks a day to push his mower,
edge crabgrass runners & pull spurge.
Doors of his old, grey International

closed around us like trashcan lids.
You couldn't roll the windows. The seat
was taped-over cotton spillage.

A boggy mat covered the floorboards
where a few marigolds & petunias rooted.
Hired at fourteen, uncollected as

the spit-cigar-shreds stuck to his truck's
inner glass, spread like disparate cities
on a back-lit map, I rolled my sleeves

over hairless arms, greased my hair
with Brylcreem, & worried, would friends
see me? Smitty's overalls hung empty

about his hips. So happy with little things —
the way he chewed his cheese sandwich,
how he beamed after he'd had a pee.

I discovered far-away sweetness
in new-mown grass. Thought it odd our
customers never greeted us. Some, wraith-like,

peeked out their windows behind remnant
tinges in their shivery curtains — pinned
notes to their screened doors, or hid them

below rocks on their porches. I came to like
his exiled work, his decrepitude of sap & loam.
I learned his unlikely grace, yard by yard.

Gareth Culshaw

On Mowing the Lawn

The petrol smoked on
pulling its heart string.
A grumbling engine, chewing
grass like a herd.

An orange tip went by
with its musical note flight
across my garden horizon.

Daisie's tickled to pop up
from regular whittling.
Dandelions shaven headed.

Mounds of blades to be raked
grass mole hills for the compost.
I turned the lawn over to a memory.

My elbows ached to press into,
knees wanted the green streaks
and burns when sliding for a ball.

We would lie under the sun,
grow with the grass. Our lives
much lighter, watching the time wave by.

Karla Linn Merrifield

Sunshine State Serpent Eating Its Tail
  ~ *for Eve Hanninen*

This world so dense with detail,
is denser still in Florida. Even
now, its silent spring so far along.

True, nothing can bring back
the splendor in the green snake
as Bartram's "innocent creature"

of his eighteenth-century Eden.
True, Archie Carr's indigo — his
extroverted "elegant product of

one hundred million years" —
its blue glory's almost gone.
Such men of densest detail are

also disappearing. Where
is an Adam for an Eve?
Would the deus-ex-machina

please send in *Stilosoma
extenuatum* the Short Tail, or
Farancia abacura the Red Belly?

A black racer would serve, too,
in this dense, detailed garden —
fading Land of Flowers.

Let there be yet a serpent's hiss,
her slither in the slick leaves
beneath live oaks

branching widely their
heavy overarching limbs,
standing in for Knowledge.

Lanette Cadle

Calculation

A rose plus thorns equals a smooth, balanced
gift, a waxy, woody stem ending in petaled splendor

minus the pricks of blood taken in payment. A daffodil
plus twenty more sprouting in the drainage ditch equals

another spring, a muddy rush of green poking through
cracked asphalt, a surprise each and every year it happens.

And it does happen. Peonies spring forth overnight. Irises
increase rhyzomatically. The redbud tree pushes aside

my fence a little more each year, and when it busts out
into bloom, its thin branches are unequal to the weight,

bending down in arcs. I should cut it down, subtract
the inevitable result of tree vs. fence, but I won't. Instead,

this year I will add a bench and when the storm clouds gather,
as they do each spring. I will sit there, not moving

under the leaves, not avoiding the rain; I will subtract my need
for reason, which will be my addition to the sum of it all.

Suzanne Sigafoos

Learning Beauty
An Apology to Conifers

    Schooled in the bare-branch,
    pink-blossom, ripe-cherry,
    falling-leaf *tao* of deciduous,
    I could not love you, spruce and cedar,

    thick against the hills, nor you,
    pines and firs, sentinels of the interstate.
    I drove fast and north then fast and south,
    dissing you as same-old-same.

    Forgive me. I am not that person now.
    I live among you, with you,
    breathing air, fresh-praised with pine,
    and in your thrall:

    you loved me when I was lost,
    love me now with ever-constant green,
    your way of stillness, willing
    to direct my eyes, every time, to the sky.

Carolyn Martin

Death of a Chinese Scholar, or Why I Had to Cut My Twelve-Year-Old Japonica Down

Japonica, aka the Chinese Scholar Tree

Of course, Confucius was first choice,
followed by Wang Wei of the Tang
and Xu Wei from the Ming.

Out-of-town … overbooked … not interested,
they said. So I recruited a young unknown
grateful for a space to grow.

A dozen years and I taught him
how to calligraph the lawn and brush paint
the fence. Soon he was translating himself:

> White-blooms-fragrancing-summer-air.
> Leaf-shade-over-rosemary-and-thyme.
> Progenitor-of-seedling-volunteers.

I loved how he grew poetry and charmed
my cat to sleep beneath the latticed leaves
that blocked my neighbor's unkempt yard.

Then late last month, the lilac bush began
to gasp for air. The weigela,
rose-of-sharon and hinoki complained.

They were right. I had ignored fine print.
A Scholar requires forty feet of height
and width. Mine was halfway there.

My chainsaw dismantled his limbs.
My rake commended leaves to recycling.
My cat sat beside herself on the patio.

Twelve years up. Two hours down.
With rueful bows of honor and respect,
I translated what he left behind:

>Half-foot-stump-framed-by-emptiness.
>Sawdust-dissolving-in-the-rain.
>Thousand-seeds-waiting-in-the-grass.

Maple Seed Pod

    O double samara
    O winged achene
    your function: diaspora

    dry fruit   drift fruit
    shaped for spinning   born
    in racemes   corymbs   umbels

    your wing elongates
    from your birdeye black satin
    seed its filmy lid laced

    and carried on the wind
    twinned   you may yet
    part company for flight

    decreasing the odds
    of getting lost   children
    pry you   sport you on their noses

    gyre   gyre   spring of life
    papery crane   maple's origami
    hundreds of thousands of you

    so they say   from one tree
    at one time   after this dream
    of flying you sleep exhausted

    sometimes for years
    before waking up
    in something else's body

Linda M. Crate

the peace the trees give

i have always
found trees
wiser, kinder
than people
always accepting my hugs
or leaning against them
allowing me to hear
the songs of birds and the caws
of crow song dancing
beneath their leaves;
never judging me for loving my feet
bare against the ground or the
gardens of vegetables, fruits, and flowers
some of which i never learned the
names;
they simply allowed me to grab their hands to
keep from falling into the creek fully
or climb upon their branches
perching like a large bird or even a wild cat —
to look across the landscape
feeling rooted in peace
was the greatest
kindness
any has granted me and i only find that sort
of tranquility when my feet are in the leaves, in the soil,
in the roots, in the petals, in the laughter
of the rain.

Rosemary Douglas Lombard

Dreaming the Delirium of Spring
(with nods to Robert Frost and Mark Strand)

1.

Still as my photograph
the cedar waits at dusk
for the promised wind,
while dollops of fine new snow cling
to the weeping branches,

ready at a breath
to fall and to blow
with the powder poised
for flight on the cluster of rooftops.

We wait, too.

2.

The blowing boughs of winter fling off the snow
in anger, as if they know their tantrums make
the graceful tip
and bow
of cherry blossoms
all the sweeter.

3.

The snow has stopped.
Under the drift on the rail
all that remains is the concrete grin
of the Cheshire tortoise,

where geraniums — now huddled close
against the wall, retreating from the Arctic air —
flowered away their summer.

4.

There is the sleep of the path not taken,
abandoned by man forever in winter.
The narcissus sleeps there
but fitfully stirs within her breaking prison.

There is the sleep of seedlings in wait,
dreaming the delirium of spring,
while camellia ponders the snow and wonders,
Shall I sleep on?

Waking Vision

they open their eyes
all of the little webs
membranes of rain
and light the instant
of that slant of morning
sun, countless matrices
seaming
various ways
the narrow distances between
telephone wires strung
one above the other
like the lacing of nerves
like the lacing of rain
and of light
crossing over
glances bordering winter
gardens, the mesh of gates
and windows, frames
uneven
interweaving
just now
shimmering
in this one way
and they open their eyes
the road black with rain
to the distances
they open their eyes
spinning
body after body
of earth and light and darkness and rain

Chamomile for the Molokans

The spider checks her web for moths
that might have strayed in dim starlight
into sticky death. She lives in the corner
above my doorway: a reminder for me
of the cycle of all things.

I watch her patch a ragged hole,
then take my shears and make my way
into the fields beyond the last porch light.
Here, the wild and tame have grown together.
Here the owl patrols on silent wings.

I've been harvesting sorrow this month,
a task best done by the dark of the moon:
angelica for protection and myrrh for mourning,
rosemary to remember, snowdrops for consolation.
And chamomile for the Molokans.

Which plant, which root or stem or flower
will give my heart song, again? Which is the herb
for breath? for moving-on?
What wreath or tea or infusion will bring about
redemption — will make up for unsaid things —

will bring back the moments, lost forever?
The light is coming up, again, turning pearl
behind the western mountains. It is time
to give-way to dawn, to return home.
Enough gathering of sorrow for one night.

Cindy Rinne

Unnamed Ghost

> *Dead bodies are buried under the sakura! You have to believe it.*
> *Otherwise, you couldn't possibly explain the beauty*
> *of the sakura blossoms.*
> *~ Motojiro Kajii (Under the Cherry Trees)*

Father, Takumi, trusted the dissonant chorus of coyote.
But only Wolf knew the moon of many petals.

Top right moon crater cupped a cherry blossom.
And then mother smells its scent, jumped back

from the buzz of bees. A month named after Mio.
Her parents at Tule Lake protested the disruption.
Mio cast a shadow at dusk.
At last her stillborn

buried in an unmarked Manzanar grave.

    fingers clutched sakura
    never held baby girl
    breasts full of milk

Diane Averill

Forms of Grief

This rock wall contains no mortar.
At the bottom, a long, sedimentary
slab, darkened with soil and moss.
It was lively with tears when I first
laid it there for Lyle, who took his
own life in a little room on Castro Street
at the beginning of the AIDS epidemic.
His closest friend, he told
his young daughter to call me first.
Next, a row of sculpted stones to represent
the dogs who were my wordless companions.
Some are broken by the weight
of that above.
A large piece of petrified driftwood
for my memory of the boy
who died building a sand cave.
I remember when he and his
brother jumped on seaweed, popping it
and try not to think of lungs under
that weight of sand and his family's
terrible grief. I wedge two whole
sand dollars between the driftwood,
and the magazine above it,
which is wrapped against the weather for my buddy, Joel,
the editor who died in Mexico. Broken
Mexican pottery instead of rocks for him.
He knew Spanish and his young lover's kiss: two tongues.

Into the hardened ash from Mt. Saint Helen's
eruption, I carve the words
mentor and *ash* for a poet-teacher I loved.
Little purple sedum brightens

in spring between some of the cracks
for the cousin who died young
of a birth defect. Laura could laugh,
love, and was loved, but was never
able to sit up or grow past the age of two.
Her name goes on in my daughter.
The heaviest rock of all I call Father,
who lived only to his late sixties
before suddenly collapsing
of a brain aneurism. A glass purple heart
goes next to his, one he received for
flying his glider onto French soil during the
Normandy invasion. The wounds he
would never talk about were shrapnel
in all of our lives. My little sister and I
slept in the same bed the night after he died.
Two small candy stripe flowers grow there.
Now I am past the age when my father died,
and I see signs of coming death in myself
and in those around me. In certain lights, those
in their late eighties turn into grey dust motes.
Aging is brutal, says Claire. One of my soul-sisters,
Pam, died of cancer. *Too soon!* Molly and I cried.
We were three, so I plant a trillium for us.
Wild sage I found slides into her river rock,
for her Portuguese hair,
green glass all around for her love of nature.

My arms are shaky, almost too old to place
my mother's igneous rock on top.
She was a drama who loved the sea. A conch goes by her,
before a sudden force I didn't know I had
pushes the whole wall over. Now I have a rock garden,
all the memories tangled together, whispering
among themselves. I mix ash into the soil so everything
grows well. Now there is room for poppies, spreading
vine-like flowers, foxglove, lupine, iris, tulips.

I throw delirious wildflower seeds everywhere
for new births. The ubiquitous *they* say I am losing
my memories, but I have so much more of them
than they could ever imagine.

Elizabeth Stoessl

Ice Plant

An infant squints into California sun
in this his first outdoor photo. The Pacific
placid behind them,
mother and child are surrounded
by a sea of succulent lushness
flowering in the sand. The mother,
native to frigid northern climes,
is astonished by February
purples, pinks and yellows.

For years, each time she returns
to this coast, she is newly enchanted
by the sight of ice plant, rampant
along the roadsides. Why not try
to grow it at home? Then, she learns
this exotic bloom is not benign: it dominates,
it conquers native plantings.
Shelter and delicacy to black rats,
its thick unchecked undergrowth
is a perfect fuel for wildfires,
demolisher of hillsides.

Sad at her discovery and disillusioned
by the spitefulness of Nature,
nonetheless the sight of these flowers still gladdens her
as it brings back the memory of that newborn boy
Kodachromed among malevolent blooms.

Amy Miller

While Deadheading Lavender, I Think of My Late Father

With my shears on a six-month strike,
this lavender shot out its last fireworks
and froze. Now there's hardly room for the living,
the dry stalks fixed and thick and clutching

dead bouquets. I grip and trace each one
and cut. But under — such a riot of green,
the embryonic buds bent on hairpin stems,
every breeze swaying their gill-tipped heads.

Crippled with a winter heart, I could only
see everything that wasn't done. But they
had started already, oils high and beading,
scent clean on blue-green arms, climbing
out of that hole into the first warm air
toward open sky and the urgent work of summer.

Kate Wells

Tending the Garden

The lavender's gone all wild and woody,
branches growing bare to the fragrant tips
and I'm outside in the slant January light
pruning the wildness back.

The shears are sharp.
The noon sun sits low
on the winter horizon.
My head is full of Mahler and Mozart,

streaming from inside the house.
That lavender scent will linger on me
long after I head in, open the darkest beer
we have in the house and sit

at the heavy wooden table in the kitchen.
The flute will take over soon,
dancing with that sweet smell
and I will finally let myself think of you.

Margaret Chula

In the Garden

Once I planted dahlia bulbs upside down. Their roots
stretched upward like albino worms, like legs of beetles
upturned by young boys who delight in their small power.

There is no pleasure in ignorance and often no punishment.

Those dahlias turned their roots around to the hard place —
toward darkness, where spring rains fell to their deepest level,
where blight could not reach nor sun blemish.

There's something pagan about dahlias — their gaudy colors,
splayed petals. Not so, the rhubarb that pokes its bulbous head
up through mud oblivious as a mole with its ruddy snout.

My grandmother welcomed their intrusions, protected them
with mulch through an uncertain spring. And when the stalks
leafed out, she cut the rhubarb with her dull and rusty knife.

I gathered the stems. They smelled of cold earth and wax.
Later, Nana and I would sit side by side at the kitchen table
and dip them into the sugar bowl.

I should have watched her: the digging, planting, and feeding.

This afternoon, I pulled up ornamental grasses, flattened
and brown, and among them green sprouts — I took those out
too, not knowing what they were until later I remembered:
purple scilla.

Like my grandmother, I welcome the soil beneath my nails
my stained and blistered palms. Today I forgive myself
for the dahlias and scilla, for everything I have made struggle.

Kay Morgan

Elegy for Emma
(September 25, 2001 - August 21, 2016)

A fledgling robin
hops the woodchipped path,
baby feathers drab camouflage,
belly barely the rusty color
it may become. Its tiny beak
peeps, calls forth a louder "cheep"

from the mother bird, diving in and out
of raised beds, zucchini, zinnias
broccoli, not unlike the Pegasus jets
practicing landings and take-offs
casting shadows over the garden,
filling the air with thunder.

The robin doesn't see her chick,
cheeps escalate. I freeze,
bystander to eventual death
if the two don't meet,
possible death even if they do.
Yet minutes ago, I crushed

the yellow larva of bean beetles
their life force pooling on lacelike
leaves, ruined by their eating.
I'm sickened – feel of the squish,
the carcass left behind –
the escalation of my attack.

Unsettled by my sudden violence,
– just or unjust – I consider
the fledgling, the larva,
who will live and who will die
on this clear blue summer day.

Roots

We pile in the car on a cool, misty Monday in the Northwest
and roll out on Thursday, crumpled and irritable
among the stubbled cornfields of the old farm —
along the swamp in southeast Missouri.
I see Mother in her straw hat, weeding the garden
with the rusty hoe she'd use to scare away
King snakes, and once a Rattler, that would hide
under the cool shade of the cucumber vines,
in the muggy mid-summer of my youth. To calm me,
she'd hold my hand and together we'd watch the slither
tracks they'd leave along the path between rows.

Mother is kneeling by the tomato plants and struggles
to stand before we even put the Subaru into park, her arms
already reaching out to fold us into her. Later, we walk
through the half block of our downtown, peer into storefronts,
long closed, climb the hill to the cemetery to set flowers
on the graves of the kids she'd lost. In the evening, we sit out
on the porch swing and face the garden, while we shell beans
and talk about the year the levee flooded, about the low price
of soybeans, about all the reasons she could never leave.
And I lean my head back, close my stinging eyes while we
sway in the soft breeze, listen to the cicadas sing in the night.

Beth Suter

Flowers Themselves

lilacs hold my earliest memories
but that is not their purpose —
their awareness is of light and shade, wet
and wind, it's a brief nectar of making,
a spreading, a quickening, they bear fruit
or they don't, unconcerned with what it means

we walk a garden of old symbols —
cherry blossoms' Zen impermanence,
Ophelia's innocent daisies and rue —
they're just cups of waiting, glistening,
they are meant for the mouths of bees and birds
the ones who eat nectar without regret

flowers grow where they find themselves, anchored
by taproot, racing each other for light
in sidewalk cracks, on desert dunes, under
dark trees, hurrying to flower and seed
while the rain lasts, while the warmth and light last
they thrive or wither, or they just abide

they are not *like* anything else —
violets, bluebells, marigolds, and pinks —
we name them by their brightest colors, yet,
they produce shades invisible to us
there's no way to know how much we can't see
we explain this with myth and religion —

Demeter's joy at Persephone's return,
an Easter lily or Buddha's lotus —
we are Narcissus, seeing only
ourselves in spring's bright mirror, painting
our human stories of resurrection
on this world of sudden, countless petals

Van Gogh Dreams of Iris

Effulgence bursts from cut-crystal.
Coddled in their bifurcated sleeve
they are not quite blue
neither are they purple.

In their minds they are orchids
birth daughters from their roots
in humus-rich Southern soil
hold the future in cupped hands.

The one-eared scarecrow twirls his brush
colors whorl, petals unfurl —
flaunt ruffled frill and fall
in interplay of tint and hue.

He hears their taffeta secrets:
perfumed hyacinths dismissed as harlots.
Lilies? My Dear, didn't you know?
Nothing but common wildflowers!

A red-headed madman tosses in sleep;
his little yellow house at Arles
tilts awkwardly askew. Iris
spin like blazing meteors.

Jeannie E. Roberts

Gardens of Light
for French Impressionist painter Oscar-Claude Monet
(1840 - 1926)

    I.

    Beneath a woodland canopy, she reads
    within a framework of filtered brilliance.
    Her bonnet bows toward her contentment.
    Dapples spill, find focus, then blur beneath
    pages. Her cloudlike raiment radiates.

    II.

    And the windswept hillside hums,
    a resplendent summer scene: son, wife,
    and nature's rousing bounty become altar,
    where her parasol shields the brightness
    of her husband's esteem.

    III.

    Subtlety sweeps with tangerine touches.
    Poppies have tipped their walk; the field
    is beige with the silver aspects of fall.
    Mother and son stroll, promenade together,
    nosegay in his grasp.

    IV.

    Bestow book, bonnet, and beatitude of day,
    where springtime is stippled and parasols
    shade, and sons gather blossoms
    for a Mommy bouquet.

Stephen Linsteadt

A Walk to the Other Side

A patch of flowers thrust their colors
to the edge of the garden

like watchdogs, anxious in anticipation.

Like a parade route, crowds of flowers lined up
on both sides of the path. I waved

as though I could hear them cheer.
Clouds lined up behind them like tethered blimps.

Birds began to sing, dogs to howl, and children darted
to the scene thinking the ruckus was the ice-cream truck.

I rushed inside to tell my wife.

She was misting her orchid,
listening to it gossip about the parade.

L. tigrinum

    The tigers have arrived
    They're all lined up, boldly striping
    the summer with the orange of their being

    Uncaged, they stand with their feet planted
    at the sunny side of the house
    They sway in the hot breeze

    If you listen carefully you can hear them
    panting   Sometimes in the soft night
    you can see their eyes glow

Stan Zumbiel

Aubade with Flowers

A green table top is piled high with gladiolus and dahlias that
she cut from the garden, walking between the rows with the shears,
clipping off long stems, shaking dew from the leaves.

She hums a dance melody and gazes deep into each blossom
connecting the shadows there with her lover. He walks
away in the cool of the morning thinking of her in a purple

dress with white lace tight around her neck, her grandmother's
cameo brightening her bodice. The flowers will sit in a smooth
green-glazed bowl over the fireplace. The light will catch

them as they exhale their fragrance, and a single petal
drops to the mantelpiece and lies like a memory — the morning
fresh from making love they rose and walked naked

through the field, came close to each other and danced away,
crossing first tilled ground then high grass that doesn't conceal her.
She doesn't care. She wants the sun to see her, wants him to see

all of her in the field glorious with their dance and bright dew.

A Beautiful Rain

You feel like a drought, yes,

but the soil does not crack
with your footsteps

nor do your bare feet
kick up dust.

Your breath does not draw
water from the dirt

or cause words
to crumble between
your teeth.

There is earth in you, yes,

but not sand. Not rock,
not desert, nothing sharp
or arid. Your edges
breathe and bend.

You pulse

in all the right
places.

There is a pool in your
heart, deep and sustaining.

Nothing has withered,
no one will drown here

or shrivel to bone.

There is storm
in your veins, yes,
but not a dry gust.

It is a beautiful rain, and
somewhere beneath it,

a field of wild grass and
tulips is spinning itself
to life.

Tone Painting

How does this season get away
with it: all the frenzied repetitions
of daffodils and daisies
madrigal of lilies
endless bards of heather
canons of buttercups
and the call and response of crickets
between Old Testament trees?

Oh, hear ye of May's pitch and satisfactions
harmonies of sun and soil
wooing boundless metaphors
of white camellia
sheltering an anaphora of pink tulips
sublimity of hyacinth and
nightingale, coo-coo and quail.

In this splendor, life and
death break bread,
an upmost wisteria rages on vine,
new leaves swoon and
prophesize pansies
and the nip and tuck of helleborus.

The neighbor child's chalk drawing
dormant on sidewalk before rain
pink rose petals sprinkled (in her self-portrait) for hair.

Flamenco Dancer

The lemon-yellow
Swallowtail butterfly
fans the garden with black tiger stripes.
Sips nectar with her crazy-straw tongue,
squeezing every drop for her two week life.
On each cabriole wing, a black teardrop
dangles like an earring.

Spindly legs twirl her skirt,
to music we don't hear.
Sun-stoked breeze strums air guitar.
Her shawl opens and flutters.
Black lace ruffles petals, shuffles pollen.

She taps her feet to the rhythm
of urge.
Her body curves
to lay eggs,
grape green pearls
that hatch in Tulip trees.

The sun melts tangerine crescents
that bead her back.
Blue sky eye shadow
smudges on black,
creased wings wink like silent castanets.

She dreams of her caterpillar days —
all those legs and false eyes
she used to fool her enemies.

She wakes from her reverie,
the scalloped hem of her wing torn,
to escape the clutch of a lizard
and dance another day.

All Wild

Though many love the topiary, boxwood,
I prefer a garden long overgrown
and spread into the wild,
wild interbreeding to reclaim ancestral ties
open pollinating freely
unconcerned with who is better
wind laying all down equally
rain drunk by all equally
verdant and effusive
floribundant and intrusive
hills all willy-nilly silly frilly
with montage-collage portages
orange lilies poking up through burgundy rhubarb
blue flax and michaelmas by wild goldenrod
for *"there is no blue without the yellow"*
michaelmas not blue nor purple nor mauve nor pewter
pincushions not lemon or lime but hued over time
milkweed and thistles
fluffing wildly like bubble machines
aromas of leaf mold, sweet earth and wild orchids
textures heaped up like thrift store clearance
colors not edited by more 'educated' eyes
burden of fleas and chiggers and bees and flies
candied nectar leaking from necks
thick alkaline poison protects
the soft and stiff and harsh and hardy
climbing all over each other in gorgeous orgy
oblivious, intertwined, without prejudice
strolled through, it and its creator
all wild
all mine

Lawn Party

Let the grass
shake loose
its green
& blaze orange
with fire
of hawkweed.
Let the grass
grow purple
heal-all, pink forget-me-nots
& wild celandine.
Let the grass
hear the violets
sing the blues,
the yowls
of white pussy-toes,
the snap-clap toe-tap
johnny jump-ups.
Let the grass
drink
the golden wine of dandelion,
raise a holy buttercup
ruckus.

Johanna Ely

Writing Poetry Is Not Like Gardening

I don't want to plant tiny seeds
that fall out of shiny packets showing
pretty pictures of daisies, marigolds, pansies.
Each kernel carefully placed and watered
inches apart from the next,
coaxed to grow and behave
the same as all the others.

I want to discover the prickly burr
that sticks to my sock,
the ochre pod caught in my hair,
the hundred dandelion seeds
clinging to my jacket like opened parachutes.
Give me something hard to pick off,
seeds that are unruly and tenacious.
Give me what survives in the dark woods,
or scrambles along a sea cliff.
Let me pull from my body
what is untamed and unsettled,
fling bright, bold words across the page,
wildflowers for the taking.

Spring Tease

Over winter-faded branches, cherry trees slip pink lace; dogwoods float daytime stars, and maples puff out yellow-green tutus.

I bloom too. Everything opens, pores, nose, mouth; and light, like the shine from pearls, fills me until giddiness tickles my stomach. So much blossoming makes me believe in forever — newly color-plumped trees will not fade into green; gray-black clouds won't rip apart the sky. Day in and day out, pink snow will drift over the asphalt; white will filigree newly minted lawns.

I should know better; I am old. But my body, not my mind, falls for spring cajoleries. *Wake up,* spring commands my skin, fall in love not just with a spring day but also with a man. The curve of my arms has utter faith that new love will shimmer until time wears out. And we will live forever. Color will not fade into green monotony and the sky will not break its promise of blue eternity.

Dianne Avey

From the Library of Mussels

We are not yet the twisted
branches of old lovers.
We are still drawn
to the scent of lilacs
and the quivering flight
of a hummingbird.

Birch bark curls
up the sides of trees.
Dogwoods open
their white palms to the sky.

In our small boat,
you dip the oars,
releasing a nautilus
of sea foam.

You are tender and patient,
like the shy plume
that tongues its way
from the barnacle.

You read to me
from the library of mussels,
and feed me the sweet cheek
of a red-red apple.

In our innocence we begin,
not knowing how steep the climb
between sea and sky.
We tell ourselves
this life will last forever.

Magnolia, After a Storm

The corner is paved with petals,
rose and pink, purple and white;
it's like walking on velvet.
I think of flower girls scattering
petals from dainty baskets,
medieval castle floors strewn
with herbs and blossoms.
I want to pick up handfuls
and lave my face with them.
A small blonde girl appears
on a pint-sized bicycle.
"Look," she says, "I found this,
and holds up a blossom, whole,
undamaged by the storm
but loosed from its branch.
"It's beautiful," we agree,
knowing without saying
that loveliness doesn't last.
One of us will grow old
sooner than the other; both
will face tempests, years
when petals litter the walk;
now they are soft underfoot.

Tassajara's Roses

I bow to the young woman inside the flower garden
as I go through the willow gate. She's the head gardener,
Felco pruners in a holster on her hip, a straw hat.

I'm a paying guest. She practices
to be a Buddhist monk.

Could I, I ask, frog-throated, *show you the way*
to prune for more rose blooms? I know roses.

She answers, *These don't produce*
many blooms. There is a great call here,
flowers for the dining room, the altars
outside the hot springs, vases in the guest rooms.
I'm an organic farmer.

There is one thing
my age knows, to feel
for both the hard nodes
in new growth that become blooms
and the mushy give of a blind shoot
that never flowers.

I ask for her pruners,
a request I know
to be like asking a samurai
to hand over a sword.
I show her when, where to cut.

Her young bloom face,
her petal hands discover
how to encourage a rose
to find more bloom.

Today's act
that outlives
the red rose.

Carolyn Martin

Notes from an August Gardener

*In the depths of winter, I finally learned that
within me there lay an invincible summer.
– Albert Camus*

Saturday morning
and not one bird makes a sound.
They're watching me
cut each gladiola down,
keeping silent in respect
for my grief over orange,
purple, white, and mottled pink.
Until next year, I relegate
each stalk to recycling.

I'm enamored with intensities
that startle and invigorate
before they slip away:
day lilies, four o'clocks,
Rose of Sharon trees,
lovers on rebound,
lightning strikes of poetry.

Still, around the yard –
patient and long-lived –
hostas, daisies, and geraniums
ride the summer out.
They'll hang on until
first frost – if affection's paid.

Just as the lid drops on
what has been, empathetic birds
turn their muteness off.

They remind me
when summer is invincible,
there's no mystery in falling,
falling in love again.

The End of the Season

Before you know what kindness is,
you must lose everything — your fertile petals,
your inner folds, the faint, mobile arc of your body.
Your fears.

Today the rain is steady. The grey mist
does not diminish the rose garden's beauty,
Blossoms, as if tumescent after a full life,
fall and scatter on the littered path.

So, too, you have bloomed and wilted
during the lush and the spare times that have
come and gone and come and gone, again.
Now, there are decisions to make,

the flurry to get things ready — just as
this shy light allows these roses
to appear timeless, radiant even,
before the last glimmer fades.

Brad G. Garber

For Their Own Good

The flowers hate it when I deadhead them
stealing the remaining beauty they offer.
"I'm not dead, yet!" they exclaim
as only flowers may upon realization of decline.

But, in their simplicity they stand beheaded
burgeoning buds prepared to fill the landscape
serpents of Medusa laughing at the sword.

Blight

You see me, your quick tears come,
and I resist the urge to flee.
Decades of dry-eyed practicality
accustomed me to the sweet serene:
the hatted gardener turning over loam,
the eternal jeans — one tear in a knee,
the second I'd spy out the window to see
as you bent to dislodge some stubborn stone.
Until one day (one night?) synapses start
to misfire, growing webcaps of plaque
instead of parsley, lady slippers, soapwort.
Your agile mind gets stranded in the muck
and soon you're all need, and for my part,
I learn to serve, getting nothing back.

Garden in Amherst

Someone whose world
has shrunk to home
still sees everything
but in a smaller grid
such as a garden,
where Emily wrote
of half-dressed hollyhocks
and agitated grass,
overloaded lilacs, blooms
that brought her closer
to death by the way
they burst into spring.
She grew from that soil
too, a shoot that watched
all the way up from its
roots while it decided
what it wanted to sing
in a season that still
hasn't stopped to this day.

Lilith

Hell, they kicked me right out of the Bible.
No one wanted to hear how I made
a killer chocolate fondue and used to
handcuff Adam to the bed. He braided my hair
while I got my nipples pierced. I painted
his toenails as a sun was tattooed
on his back. He's shy of that now, won't show
anyone, but I know all about it. Oh, he won't
tell you how we stayed up late talking, spiking
each other's hair. How we popped corn
and threw it at the moon — and all those nights,
crows upon crows at our feet. He likes to forget
we used to make up songs together, flinging
lines at each other, splashing in the claw-foot tub.
We planted a garden that bloomed
unlikely things — the artichoke mingling
with the birds, the snap peas tangling threads
to spell out wishes. The weed I pulled and pulled
that wouldn't give until I dug, found its claws
wrapped around a stone. Together we picked
tomatoes, green and young, watched them
turn somersaults in our wicker basket. Dreadlocked
carrots, weeping leeks, the pumpkin spreading
wider than our house! And how we cooked and cooked,
turned spices in butter, tamed vegetables, licked
the spoons, ate off each other's plates. And always
the scent of lilacs, cherry blossoms, coaxing us
into the blue of night, the perfect relief of stars.
We'd walk the dogs down the road
to the abandoned silo, make love in the grain
until the sun slipped through the roof. Or
lie naked in the forgotten treehouse, listening
to acorns falling from the sky. It was all about

how much we wanted to slip inside each other,
find our way up and down our bodies' bones.
Until I found the missing rib.
I noticed it gone, then saw he'd planted it
in the garden. She grew taller than the rhubarb,
taller than me. I put my hands on my hips
and hollered: Take her, but leave me
the dogs, leave me the garden.
You'll never find *this* again.
But someday she'll come walking, she'll see
this garden and reach for something here.
I'll watch her from the kitchen window.
I'll let her take whatever she likes.
And when she does, you'll crumble.
You'll turn on your heels
and run.

Queens Kitchen

    Heat-crazed Salinas soil
        crackles. Beyond, the Coast Range
            shimmers a blue mirage. Workers
                wade through

the dry ripples, balancing
    a crate of sun on their backs
        like lost shore birds

searching beneath serrated
    leaves for seed-pocked berries
        tapered to a nub between thumb
            and finger, drooping

as sweat drips, mocking the memory
    of rain. The fields shrivel
        to scant penciled furrows.

In a clean, white kitchen
    someone will taste this harvest, more
        salt than sweet. Grit.
            Fruit, a future myth.

Tim Kahl

Dynasty Dandelion

After three years of drought
the yard returns to the wild,
the fine-trimmed lawn gives way to
bare patches of ground where the dogs
lie down and cool their pads.
It is the era of neglect, the weed
on the flag of Dynasty Dandelion.
I go out to manage the display
but my heart's not into taming
the uncouth growth that's climbing
the fence, strangling the plum.
All that I survey is furious with
its own happening. A seedling from
last season's fruit fall has sprouted.
The fig's root has displaced the garden's
berm and the aging dog shit has
dressed itself in the most curious mold.
It's like the hair of a troll announcing
it is coming out. So I take notice.
I imagine where I might place the part,
half of the hair running towards
the elegant pot of mint, the other half
angled at the chair where the stray
lifted its leg. How terrified that little guy
was and no welcoming lick when
he saw his owner again. There are stranger
foes than a little overgrowth out there.
There's a lot of weeding to be done
in the rooms where people talk
and wait. They expect the night
to come and help them sort it all out,
but no one can garden when the moon
glows its lonely castaway soul.

Scott A. Russell

Ecliptical Allegory

Four views
of a cider lit garden,
late afternoon:

>the scientist squints through
>a flapping rectangle of night
>for the universe in pinprick,
>a literal microcosm, while

>the activist disdains
>her camera obscura
>for direct action,
>scalding her retinas.

>The poet admires the abstract
>spangling of little smiles,
>pocketing a few for later as

>the caregiver caroms
>between the other three,
>seeing the light
>only refracted, diminished,
>defined by what it has lost.

Unnoticed by each, the glorious gestalt —
time made visible
as a gossamer of
innumerable crescents
drawn leisurely down over
stucco and brick, bracken and bark,
a palimpsest of gold upon green.

Irene Bloom

Once in a Blue Moon

On this night, too hot to sleep,
I am on the patio at 2 a.m.
feet in a bucket of ice water.

Even the glare of the moon
pours the sun's reflection onto the patio.
Is there no escaping this constant dazzle
of light, this eternal radiance, even after dark?

Here in my little courtyard
all is illuminated. Tiny orbs
of potted tomatoes shine like cherry gems,
the small pond of a birdbath
aglow like molten glass.

On this night that singular satellite
is full again — twice in one month.
They call it a blue moon.
But tonight it radiates
the brightest of white light.

This night this supermoon,
is closest to Earth in it's eternal orbit.
Looking up, we are nearer than ever —
me and my swollen feet cooling in the bucket
and that man up there, his familiar face
shining down so close and clear.

This time his undeniable grin
seems to speak to me. He tells me

Take care my dear, your planet is burning.

Sherry Wellborn

The Indictment of Flowers

Some years it is only the flowers that call.
The peonies and the moon-faced clematis,
drifts of yellow alliums and poppy capsules
are the needed nourishment
for me and the bombyliid and hoverflies.
Let the ideological vegetables take a powder.
Forget the locavore asparagus
and the nutrient-dense organically fertilized potatoes.
I need the floozies,
the pole dancers in erotic petals,
over-perfumed Damasks,
night-scented angel's trumpets,
a flood of bloodied crocosmia spikes,
daggers of devil's club,
even the musk of skunk cabbage.
In summer's dry heat I will focus
on lavender and the clear yellow candelabras of *Phlomis*.
Perhaps my mouth will miss cucumbers,
but my eyes will gulp down purple and pearly pink,
my fingers will pet the *Knifophia* for nectar,
my nose will wallow in lily pollen.
There are the irrepressible raspberries should my tongue complain.
And if climate change inches forward
because of my flower thirst,
so be it.
I accept responsibility for
the end of the world.

Kenneth Pobo

Farfugium with Exclamation Point

As August aches into September,
I cling to every remaining bloom.
Some are more fulsome
than ever — giant marigolds,
tall Mexican sunflowers.
You'd think autumn was a rumor
easily disproved. October comes
more quickly than I imagined.
Aster time. Goldenrod.

November, I rub fading asters
and a roulette coreopsis
by the road. December,
the garden has closed its eyes
for the last time. Except —

a farfugium! Small daisy-like
yellow petals in a barrel
near the garage. On our way
to work, we pull out woolen scarves.
The flower tips her hat
to a gray sky, large green leaves
shining when all hope
seemed to go poof.

Michael Baldwin

After Election Day
(November 2016)

The sudden autumn chill astonished the trees,
quickly stripped them, betrayed leaves scattering in panic,
presumptuous celebratory colors soon blanching,
some clotted in my ornamental pond, clogging the pump,
many more caught up in momentary whirlwinds, then
collapsing, massing against fences, chattering and scuffling,
waiting apprehensively to be piled for composting.
Skeletal trees, now naked to the ravening wind,
shiver and thrash gracelessly.
The little birds seek asylum amid low, prickly bushes
that offer no safety from minatory hawks.
A plump orange squirrel wanders imperiously
among this carnage and confusion,
burying pecans, plundering birdseed.

The Remembrance Poppy

The gardener bathes the poppies
daily as new shoots sprout
from the sleeping roots to
honor their honeycomb treaty.

Each emerald rendition
strung like vertebrae,
is capped with cherry bonnets
and an ash dimple of earth.

The most courageous of petaled
ascenders stem from their fallen
former selves and give their
stalks in memoriam for country.

Steve Williams

If We Hadn't Lost Eden

Garden *noun, (gar-den)*

1a: A plot of ground where herbs, fruits, flowers, or vegetables are cultivated.

Not a row of maples planted in rectangular holes in the sidewalk,
not a field of strawberries or Christmas trees,
not a dog park full of tail joy and necessity,
not the war memorial, the rose on the casket.

1b: A rich well-cultivated region.

Not New Jersey, not the Napa valley, not poppies or cocoa leaves,
not the Barrier Reef or anything else in the sea,
not Mauna Loa, Vesuvius, or St. Helens,
not the Parthenon, the Vatican, or the Mayans.

1c: A container (as a window box) planted usually with a variety of small plants.

Not silk flowers or plastic leaves,
not the terrarium, the rusty wheelbarrow,
not digging potatoes or pulling carrots
but rather what you empty out of a plastic bag.

2a: A public recreation area or park usually ornamented with plants and trees (a botanical garden).

Not a wildlife refuge, not gathering shells broken by the beaks of gulls,
not driftwood or the remains of a campfire,
not anything in a wild river, not the boat ramp,
not the peregrine chick falling from the nest on the bridge,
perhaps to fly.

2b: An open air eating or drinking place.

Not a sidewalk café, a rooftop reception,
not the grilled cheese food cart, not the baseball game,
not the end of the pilgrimage or any refugee camp,
not the rest area on the freeway, not the road kill.

2c: A large hall for public entertainment.

Not any casino, theater, or strip club, not a convention hall,
not Walmart, not the opera, symphony, ballet or any type of museum,
not a gallery, a cruise ship, or any library,
not a pipe organ, a hymnal, a cross.

Not any place that will help us forget.

In This Garden

    I am the wind that whips your hair
    across your face, covering eyes
    as you strip bare winter's waste.

    I am the soil beneath your fingernails
    the roots that won't budge, the sludge.

    I am a whisper — my wondrous words
    are words of wisdom heard from within
    as you pull bothersome weeds. They tell you

    hands like yours were meant to toil even though
    some say this world is full of weeds, why bother?

    You will listen to me because when we are here
    together in this garden, you hear me. I help you
    forget about college tuition, middle age, Trump.

    In the moment, we worry not about things
    we cannot change, but what we can.

Viola Weinberg

Today, I Will Only Attend to the Small Things

The tiny basil flowers, for instance
that I will pinch back for the sake of the plant
The little carrots deliciously ready, but very short
The one beet that stands alone in its bed
bursting from the soil, red and bleeding
The last French radish, which has gotten
rather large, but can still be sliced
in two and set in a water bath to crisp
or the dead heads of carnations on a plant
that once looked like an explosion of red paint

My plans involve the garden shears and clippers
grown gamy now from pruning sappy limbs
or watching the little dog, who lies in the sun, still
as the sleeping Buddha or the pea shoots
trying to latch on the old willow teepee
or the little figlets still shapeless and vague —
but surely ready to be counted, their perfume
preceding their womanly bodies, their forming seed
I will rediscover the lost glove with a patch
and measure the cucumbers just set in a row

I will not think about things so big they are unimaginable:
Death, dearth, why some are loved and some are not
I will continue my subtle movements, small and tender
As if they were cilia in the ear of a thirsty honey bee
In this small world, I shall gather, cut, water and harvest
Entire life cycles of their little universe of mulch and dirt
I will hum a modest tune and clip the ragged thyme
No one will be saved; there is no winner's bell to ring —
just the soft breeze with an insinuation of the ocean
a small planet of things to tend, one sleepy clover at a time

Gently On My Mind
(a cascade)

Silence is broken by lovely birdsong.
I waken to take in the twilight at four.
Mysterious rotation without hesitation.
The world rests gently on my mind.

Mayflies and June bugs dance lively fandangos
by porch lamp and streetlight post's luminous glow.
Cool humidity softens spring darkness
when silence is broken by lovely birdsong.

Dog out the back door and cat in the front door,
the dew on the grass as they pass wets their paws
and makes tracks on the floor as they come in to eat.
I waken to take in the twilight at four.

Soothing libation and strong medication
with stretching to meditate body and soul
while earth on its journey, determined, goes forth;
mysterious rotation without hesitation.

Iris, alyssum and grape vines all bloom
in the turquoise shadows of the breaking dawn
on a beautiful day still so early in May and
the world rests gently on my mind.

Blaze

Suddenly the peonies are too much for themselves — heavy-headed,
huge and falling — not spent, but wildly spending
utter color, unfurling perfume, sure and reckless lavish.
May I come through like this someday,
come through to a vastness on my feet and running,
the old cart of thought abandoned on the road,
and love — the heat, the secret way across the border — laying me bare.

Cathy Cain

Therefore Eternal

With a hoot and a holler, I allow lusty clichés,
vigorous in their tenacity, to course through my mind.

I do not wish to number my days
this clean, cool morning, as I sit in my garden chair,

but rather let them flow just out of control,
as each day evolves,

materializes from naught.
Immaculate conception.

Under these layered branches, the leaves rustle.
Sunlight suddenly visits, takes my wrist.

Linda Ferguson

And on Earth, the Garden of the Universe

And on Earth, the garden of the universe, some walked with snowy birds on their shoulders, and some pierced the breasts of scarlet birds to show who was boss, and some stretched and inhaled the scent of morning jasmine, and some stepped over the sweet stench of rotting flesh, and some wore veils and whispered their daily prayers under the peach trees, and some flung off their veils and raised their fists to the unblinking sky, and some marched and shouted at those who wouldn't march and shout with them, and some swatted the bees whose drones interrupted their dreams, and some manufactured golden apples in the test tubes of white laboratories, and some built cars that could turn the blossoms of the garden into a blur, and some said 'no more,' and some said 'more, more,' and some cursed the bleating of sheep, and some cursed the screech of eagles, and some cursed the keening of coyotes, and some purchased plots of the garden and divided those plots into micro-plots and sold each micro-plot for a taste of chocolate, and some slept in towers that pricked the stars, and some slept under the tinkling rain of stalactites, and some slept on warm sands that conformed to the curves of their spines, and some leapt from cliffs and tried to fly, and some dynamited tunnels to seek diamonds to sew into the linings of their coats, and some never looked another creature in the eye, and some swooned at the sound of a voice on the radio, and some sharpened their claws, and some shaved their hair and some braided their hair and some frosted their hair and some painted their hands and some lifted their breasts and some chopped off their toes and some stretched their earlobes and some rearranged their ribs and some bleached their teeth and some bleached their skin and some powdered their wigs, and some wove armor out of shards of bone and dried grass, and some danced on ponds of glass, and some made laws that said 'no music,' and some met their lovers in the shadows of conifers, and some burned the conifers for fuel, and some made sculptures they tucked under ferns, and some murmured poems beneath the brooks, and some made signs that spelled their own names in electric lights, and some kissed for the joy of kissing and some kissed out of curiosity and some kissed from a sense of duty and some kissed because their lips were cold and some kissed to keep the kissees from speaking, and some picked all the pears and stored them behind secret doors, and some scooped up all the salmon, and some shared the last olive with a distant cousin and some offered a drop of wine to a gleaming stranger, and some strung pearls of rain and wore them like a crown, and some climbed sequoias and proclaimed themselves monarchs, and some loved the monarchs like a mother, and some ignored the monarchs and kept kissing, and some bowed to the monarchs then mocked them when the monarchs were out of earshot, and some monarchs learned how to bake bread and some monarchs learned how to stoke fires and some monarchs learned how to grow flowers and some monarchs learned how to kill lions, and some of their subjects warned that the garden would die if everyone didn't bless it with seeds and tears, and some threw stones at those who issued warnings, and some lay awake at night listening for their instructions in the silence, and some offered arias to empty skies, and some drew plans for ships that could take them to a place where they could start another garden, and we all took our first icy breaths on Earth, the garden of the universe, and we all trembled at the thought of death, even when we believed it was just a story that was sure to end happily.

Acknowledgments

We gratefully acknowledge the following publications in which these poems first appeared:

"Fertilized by Mark Strand" by Ada Jill Schneider was previously published in *Fine Lines and Other Wrinkles* (Gratlau Press).

"Recycling in a Well-Tended Garden" by Tricia Knoll first appeared on *US Represented*, September 2015.

"Learning Beauty" by Suzanne Sigafoos first appeared in *The Sunday Oregonian*, in 2012.

"L. tigrinum" by Phyllis Wax was previously published in *Free Verse* #96, July 2008.

"Tassajara's Roses" by Tricia Knoll was published on *Verse-Virtual*, March 2015.

A modified version of "The End of the Season" by Marilyn Johnston was published in *Write the Town 2016* (Salem, OR: Mid-Valley Poetry Society, December 2016), under the title "At Gaiety Hollow."

"The Indictment of Flowers" by Sherry Wellborn was published in *How to Love Everything*, a chapbook produced by Red Sofa Poets, 2015.

Contributors

Ada Jill Schneider, winner of the National Galway Kinnell Poetry Prize, is the author of four volumes of poetry. She directs "The Pleasure of Poetry" at the Somerset Public Library in Massachusetts. Ada started writing poetry at the age of fifty-three when she thought she was old. <www.adajillschneider.com>

Alec Solomita wrote his first poem at 14 and has remained undissuaded from persevering in this sometimes thankless activity. His fiction has appeared in several publications. He's published poetry in *Literary Orphans, Silver Birch Press, The Poeming Pigeon*, and elsewhere. He lives in Somerville, Mass. <solomitaalec@gmail.com>

After several decades spent among the backwoods of Kentucky, **Allison Thorpe** is now navigating the wilds of city life. The author of several collections of poetry, she has recent work in *Still: The Journal, So To Speak*, and *Hamilton Stone Review*. She is working on her first novel.

Alwyn Marriage's eight books include four poetry collections and she's widely represented in magazines, anthologies and on-line. Formerly university philosophy lecturer, Director of international NGOs and Rockefeller Scholar, she's currently Managing Editor of Oversteps Books and research fellow at Surrey University. <www.marriages.me.uk/alwyn>

Amy Miller's writing has appeared in *Nimrod, Rattle*, and ZYZZYVA. One of her first published pieces was an essay on renting houses and leaving gardens behind. When she opened the letter from *Fine Gardening* saying they had accepted it, she was so surprised that she actually fell down. <writers-island.blogspot.com>

Ann Howells edits *Illya's Honey*, recently taking it digital: www.IllyasHoney.com. Her publications are: *Black Crow in Flight* (Main Street Rag Publishing), *Under a Lone Star* (Village Books Press), *Letters for My Daughter* (Flutter Press), and *Cattlemen & Cadillacs,* an anthology of D/FW poets she edited (Dallas Poets Community Press).

Annie Lighthart is a writer and teacher who started writing poetry after her first visit to an Oregon old-growth forest. Poems from her book *Iron String* have been read on *The Writer's Almanac*, have been placed in hospitals in Ireland and New Zealand, and have traveled farther than she has. <www.annielighthart.com>

Barbara A. Meier is really just a farm girl from Kansas who now looks at Pacific waves instead of waves of grain. She teaches Kindergarten and First graders in Gold Beach, OR. Her poem, "Glass Jar Memories," appeared in *The Poeming Pigeon* a year ago. <Basicallybarb@gmail.com>

Beth Suter studied Environmental Science at U.C. Davis and has worked as a naturalist and teacher. She is also an award-winning poet and a Pushcart Prize nominee, with recent or forthcoming pieces in *American Tanka*, *Sacramento Voices*, and *Albatross*. She lives in Davis, California with her husband and son.

Brad G. Garber writes, paints, draws, photographs, hunts for mushrooms and snakes, and runs around naked in the Great Northwest. Since 1991, he has published poetry, essays and weird stuff in such publications as *Embodied Effigies*, *Clementine Poetry Journal*, *Barrow Street*, *Aji Magazine* and other quality publications. 2013 Pushcart Prize nominee. <bggarber@yahoo.com>

After a dozen years on the West Coast, **Brigit Truex** has once again relocated in the "mid-East" of the country, one state in from the coast. Among her publications are her most recent book, *Strong as Silk*, as well as four chapbooks and numerous journals and anthologies. <brigittruex@gmail.com>

Brittney Corrigan is the author of the poetry collections *Navigation* and *40 Weeks*. Her poems have appeared widely in journals, and she is poetry editor for *Hyperlexia: poetry and prose about the autism spectrum*. Brittney lives in Portland, Oregon, where she is both an alumna and employee of Reed College. <https://brittneycorrigan.com/>

C. Hunter Davis shares thin clay soil with slugs, deer and one plump raccoon and manages to grow lupines. She first wrote in fourth grade when she learned more looking out the window than at the teacher. Her poems have been published in *Echoes*, *Island of Geese and Stars*, and *Ferry Tales*. <cahunda@aol.com>

Carolyn Martin gardens, writes, and plays in Clackamas, Oregon. Her poems and book reviews have been published throughout the US and UK, and her second collection, *The Way a Woman Knows*, was released by The Poetry Box in 2015. <portlandpoet@gmail.com>

A founder of Airlie Press, **Carter McKenzie** is the author of the chapbook *Naming Departure* and a book of poetry *Out of Refusal*. Her poems have most recently appeared in *Turtle Island Quarterly*. Carter's poem "The Coffin of Emmett Till" was nominated for a Pushcart Prize in 2015. <cartermck@epud.net>

Catherine McGuire has 3 decades of poetry in publications like *New Verse News, FutureCycle, Portland Lights, Fireweed,* and on a bus for *Poetry In Motion.* She has four chapbooks, including *Glimpses of a Garden,* and a full-length book of poetry, *Elegy for the 21st Century* (FutureCycle Press). <www.cathymcguire.com>

Cathy Cain is a writer, painter, and printmaker living in Oregon. Her honors include the Kay Snow 2016 Paulann Petersen Poetry Award from Willamette Writers; the 2015 Edwin Markham Prize for Poetry from *Reed Magazine;* and recognition from the Oregon Poetry Association.

Cheryl A. Van Beek is grateful to have won poetry contests with *Creative Writing Ink* and to have had poems published with *Sandhill Review, River Poets Journal* and many others. She lives with her wonderful husband and their two cats in Florida—The Land of Flowers. <cvanbeek@tampabay.rr.com>

Cindy Rinne creates art and writes in San Bernardino, CA. Cindy is the author of several books. She is a founding member of PoetrIE, a literary community and a finalist for the 2016 Hillary Gravendyk Prize poetry book competition. Her poetry appeared in many literary magazines. <www.fiberverse.com>

Claudine Nash's poetry collections include *Parts per Trillion* (Aldrich Press, 2016) and *The Problem with Loving Ghosts* (Finishing Line Press, 2014). Her poetry has won numerous prizes and has appeared in such publications as *Asimov's Science Fiction, Cloudbank* and *Haight Ashbury Literary Journal.* She is also a practicing psychologist. <www.claudinenashpoetry.com>

Daniel Williams is a poet of the Sierra/Yosemite region of California. His work has appeared in many publications, including a haiku engraved on the Maven Martian explorer and poems in Yosemite's time capsule to be opened in the year 2140. <yosepoet@msn.com>

Diane Averill has published four books of poems. Two were finalists for the Oregon Book Award. One was listed as one of The 26 Best Poems in Oregon. Her most recent magazine publications are *The Bitter Oleander* and *Voicecatcher.*

Dianne Avey lives on a small island in southern Puget Sound and usually writes her poetry while commuting on the ferry. Her poetry has appeared in *Pulse, Wrist Magazine, The Poeming Pigeon,* and others. <dianneavey@gmail.com>

Elizabeth Stoessl's poetry has been widely published in journals and anthologies, among them *Measure, Poetica,* and *Sow's Ear Poetry Review*. Her relocation from Northern Virginia to Portland, Oregon, has been a happy transition, though she misses the backyard gardens she left behind, and now contents herself with summertime balcony plantings. <estoessl@gmail.com>

Emily Pittman Newberry's writing explores the challenges of living as spiritual beings in a material world. OneSpirit Press published two of her books; she wrote the poetry for the artist Shu-Ju Wang's artist's book *Water;* and she was nominated for a Pushcart Prize in 2014. <www.butterflyarose.com>

Eric le Fatte was educated at MIT and Northeastern University in biology and English, but currently teaches, hikes, and writes in Portland, Oregon. He has published in *Rune, Mountain Gazette, Windfall, Clackamas Literary Review, Raven Chronicles, Perceptions,* and *Cirque*; and received the Oregon Poetry Association's Spring 2015 New Poet's Award. <elef1234@gmail.com>

Gareth Culshaw lives in Wales. He is an aspiring writer who hopes one day to achieve something with the pen. <jaspers1980@aol.com>

Georgette Howington, naturalist, horticulturist, freelance writer and poet lives minimally in a small house and grows vegetables, flowers and herbs in two community gardens nearby. Her poems have been published in *Poeming Pigeons, Iodine,* and recently, awarded Honorable Mention for the 2016 Ina Coolbrith Circle contest. <www.gardenboheme.com>

Heather Angier's poetry has appeared in many journals, including *ZYZZYVA,* which she usually mentions because they paid her 50 bucks. She is the author of two chapbooks: *Crooked* (Dancing Girl Press) and *Nest* (Finishing Line Press). She has an MFA in English and Creative Writing from Mills College. <hangier@sbcglobal.net>

Irene Bloom is an emerging poet from Seattle, Washington whose work is inspired by her world travels, love of language, and sharing the written word with others. Her poems have appeared in *Kind of a Hurricane Press, Poetica Magazine, Cirque,* and other national and international publications. <bloomwrite@gmail.com>

James B. Nicola has appeared previously in *The Poeming Pigeon* and recently in the *Southwest* and *Atlanta Reviews, Poetry East,* and *Rattle*. His nonfiction book

Playing the Audience won a Choice award. His two poetry collections (Word Poetry) are *Manhattan Plaza* (2014) and *Stage to Page: Poems from the Theater* (2016). <sites.google.com/site/jamesbnicola.>

Now an old lady, **Janet M. Powers** is still writing poems and seeing them in print after 50 years of college teaching. She enjoys pottering in her garden, dabbling in photography and publishing in journals such as *Antietam Review*, *Earth's Daughters* and *Pamplemousse*. <jpowers0135@earthlink.net>

Jeannie E. Roberts writes, draws and paints, and often photographs her natural surroundings. Her fifth book, *The Wingspan of Things*, a poetry chapbook, is forthcoming from Dancing Girl Press. She is the author of *Beyond Bulrush*, a full-length poetry collection (Lit Fest Press, 2015). <jeannie.roberts@jrcreative.biz>

Jennifer Lagier has published thirteen books and in literary magazines, taught with California Poets in the Schools, co-edits the *Homestead Review*, and helps coordinate Monterey Bay Poetry Consortium Second Sunday readings. Newest books: *Scene of the Crime* (Evening Street Press), *Harbingers* (Blue Light Press), *Camille Abroad* (FutureCycle Press). <jlagier.net>

Johanna Ely's poetry has been published in several anthologies and online journals, and recently, in *California Quarterly*. In 2015, she published a small collection of poetry titled *Transformation*. Johanna is honored to be the current poet laureate of Benicia, California. Her favorite garden is the Japanese Garden in Portland, Oregon. <jelyabc13@yahoo.com>

John Davis is the author of *Gigs* and *The Reservist*. His work has appeared recently in *DMQ Review* and *One*. He adores stinging nettle soup, peaches, and playing harmonica in a blues band.

Judith Skillman's recent book is *Kafka's Shadow*, Deerbrook Editions. Her work has appeared in *Cimarron Review*, *Shenandoah*, *FIELD,* and elsewhere. Awards include an Eric Mathieu King Fund grant from the Academy of American Poets. Skillman has done collaborative translations from French, Portuguese, and Macedonian. <www.judithskillman.com>

A nine-time Pushcart-Prize nominee and National Park Artist-in-Residence, **Karla Linn Merrifield** has twelve books to her credit, the newest of which is *Bunchberries: More Poems of Canada*, a sequel to. *Godwit: Poems of Canada* (FootHills). She is assistant editor/poetry book reviewer for *The Centrifugal Eye*. <klmerrifield@yahoo.com>

Kate Wells tends to the future by teaching English at a high school in California. She has been published in *Ash Canyon Review*, *Rattlesnake Review*, and *Words of Wisdom*.

Kay Morgan's poetry has been published recently in the anthologies *Piscataqua Poems*, *Poet's Showcase* and *Verse Osmosis*. During the summer she may be found tending her plots in the Wagon Hill Community Garden. She lives and writes in the Seacoast of New Hampshire. <morgan.katherin@comcast.net>

Katy Brown, a retired social worker, poet, and photographer, whose work appears online and in numerous journals and anthologies, has won a ton of impressive awards in various competitions; has twice been nominated for the Pushcart Prize. She grew up with hawks, rattlesnakes, and an older brother. <kbrown4081@aol.com>

Kelila A Knight is an MFA candidate at Oklahoma State University. Her poetry has appeared in *If You Can Hear This: Poems in Protest of an American Inauguration*.

Kenneth Pobo loves to garden. Garden 2016 provided fabulous lilies and several boffo dahlias. Failures too--it wouldn't be a garden without them, like our Tom Edison dahlia, critter-eaten. Book coming out in 2017 from Circling Rivers: *Loplop in a Red City*. <@KenPobo (Twitter)>

Lanette Cadle teaches rhetoric and creative writing at Missouri State University in Springfield, just down the road from that shrine to pop culture and outlet shopping, Branson. She has previously published poetry in *TAB: The Journal of Poetry and Poetics*, *Yellow Chair Review*, *Rose Red Review*, *Stirring*, and *By&By Poetry*. <poet.lanettecadle.com>

Larry Schug lives with his wife and three cats and one dog near a large tamarack bog between St. Joseph and St. Wendel, Minnesota. <www.larryschugpoet.com>

Laurie Kolp is the author of *Upon the Blue Couch* (Winter Goose Publishing, 2014) and *Hello, It's Your Mother* (Finishing Line Press, 2015). Her recent publications include concis, *By&By Poetry*, *Bracken*, *Up the Staircase Quarterly*, *Front Porch Journal*, and more. Laurie lives in Texas with her husband and children. <lauriekolp.com>

Laurinda Lind is no kind of gardener in northern New York, though for a few years, pumpkins grew unaided and uninvited out from under her front porch. In honor of *The Poeming Pigeon*, here are some poetry publications and acceptances that start with P: *Passager, Plainsongs,* and *Paterson Literary Review.* <lpetersen@sunyjefferson.edu>

Lillo Way's poems have appeared or are forthcoming in *New Orleans Review, Poet Lore, Tar River Poetry,* among others. Seven of Way's poems are included in anthologies. Long an apartment dweller, Way recently moved to a house with a small garden. <lilloway@gmail.com>

Linda Ferguson is an award-winning writer of poetry, fiction and essays. Her poetry chapbook, *Baila Conmigo,* was published by Dancing Girl Press. She also teaches writing for adults and children, and her heart soars every summer when the purple Echinacea she started from seed reappears. <www.bylindaferguson.blogspot.com>

Linda M. Crate's writing has appeared in many magazines both online and in print. Her latest chapbook is *If Tomorrow Never Comes* (Scars Publications, August 2016) and *Centaurs & Magic* is her latest novel. < www.facebook.com/Linda-M-Crate>

Liz Nakazawa is the editor of two anthologies of poems by Oregon poets: *Deer Drink the Moon: Poems of Oregon* and *The Knotted Bond: Oregon Poets Speak of Their Sisters.* Her poetry and haiku has appeared in *The Timberline Review,* the poetry anthology, *Turn,* and *ahundredgourds.*

M. Wright received his bachelor's degree in English from the University of Minnesota and is the winner of Weisman Art Museum's "Poetry ArtWords" 2015. His poems have been published in several online and print publications and in 2017 he will be featured in the *Saint Paul Almanac*'s "Impressions Project" series. <wrightm.com>

Margaret Chula lived in Kyoto for twelve years where she taught creative writing at universities. Her eight poetry collections include, most recently, *Daffodils at Twilight.* She has been a featured speaker and workshop leader at writers' conferences and festivals throughout the United States, as well as in Poland, Canada, and Japan. <www.margaretchula.com>

Marilyn Johnston is a Salem writer and filmmaker. She received a writing fellowship from Oregon Literary Arts and was the winner of the Donna J. Stone

National Prize for Poetry. She is a writing instructor in the Artists in the Schools Program, primarily working with incarcerated youth. <mejohnston100@gmail.com>

Matt Farr is an advertising writer, lover of beer, fixer of faucets, and driver of kids. The documentary on his life was canceled when the director fell asleep during the read-through. Nevertheless, it's been a good run so far. <mattfarr@gmail.com>

Michael Baldwin is an award-winning poet and novelist, who has published three collections of poetry. His poetry was featured on the national radio program, *The Romantic Hours*, and has twice been considered for The Pushcart Prize. He is a former librarian and professor of American Government, residing in Benbrook, Texas. <librmike@hotmail.com>

G. Murray Thomas is a Southern California poet with a brown thumb. He has grown one successful garden in his life, and this poem is about that garden. <gmurraythomas.com>

Neil Creighton is an Australian poet who says gardening keeps him sane. Find him in his veggie patch, little orchard or the meandering paths of his bush garden. His recent publications include *Poetry Quarterly* and *Praxis Online Mag*. He is a contributing editor at *Verse-Virtual*. <windofflowers.blogspot.com.au>

Pamela Ahlen is currently program coordinator for Bookstock, The Green Mountain Literary Festival. She organizes literary readings for Osher (Lifelong Education at Dartmouth). Pam received an MFA in creative writing from Vermont College of Fine Arts. She is the author of the chapbook *Gather Every Little Thing* (Finishing Line Press).

Pattie Palmer-Baker is an artist and poet. Over the years of exhibiting her artwork — a combination of paste paper collages and poetry in calligraphic form — she discovered that most people like poetry; in fact many liked her poems better than the visual art. She now concentrates on writing. <PattiePalmerBaker.com>

Paul Yager is a poet and retired architect. He was a runner up in the Cambridge Sidewalk Poetry contest and studies poetry with Barbara Helfgott Hyett. Of all his projects he claims that his best ones are his grown children, Josh and Abby, and his granddaughter, Miru Pearl. <paulyagerpoetry@gmail.com>

Phyllis Wax writes in Milwaukee on a bluff overlooking Lake Michigan. A Pushcart Prize nominee, her poetry has appeared in *Ars Medica, Naugatuck River Review* and *The New Verse News,* as well as many other journals and anthologies, print and online. Every January she takes part in a poetry marathon. <poetwax38@gmail.com>

Rachelle M. Parker is a Callaloo Creative Writing Fellow. Her poetry has appeared in *Tupelo Quarterly, Creations Magazine, The Path Magazine, Elohi Gadugi* and the anthology *The Poeming Pigeon: Poems About Food.* She was the winner of the Pat Schneider Poetry Contest 2014. Rachelle is currently the poetry editor for *Peregrine: the literary journal of Amherst Writers and Artists.*

Robert Eastwood is a Scorpio with all the trappings. His work recently appeared in *The Kentucky Review, Halfway Down The Stairs,* and *Steel Toe Review.* He has three chapbooks that few people read by Small Poetry Press. His first book, *Snare,* was recently published by Broadstone Press. <boble38@sbcglobal.net>

Animal behaviorist/writer/poet **Rosemary Douglas Lombard** and her lab turtles love their wild, fruit-filled garden. Lombard's literary work appears in *Bay Nature, Verseweavers,* and chapbook *Turtles All the Way: Poems* (Finishing Line Press). <ChelonianConnection.blogspot.com>

Ruth Hill was raised in upstate New York, and traveled North America extensively. She is a Certified Design Engineer, tutor, and enjoys spoken word. Over 250 of her poems have won awards or publication in the US, Canada, UK, Australia, and Israel. <ruthhill@joiedevivregardens.ca>

Scott A. Russell is a poet, husband, and father, and a fancier of all things fried or frivolous. <s.a.russellpoetry@gmail.com>

Sara Wilson is a graduate of Vancouver Island University, earning her BA with a major in Creative Writing. Her poems have appeared in *Dinosaur Porn, Slim Volume,* and *White Stag.* She is a Red Seal Sheet Metal Journeywoman and a novice cellist. <sarawilsonpoet.wordpress.com>

Shari Jo LeKane-Yentumi (B.A./M.A. English/Spanish - Saint Louis University) lives in St. Louis, Missouri, and writes articles, literary critiques, poetry and prose. With a novel in verse, *Poem to Follow,* and a book of poetry, *Fall Tenderly,* Shari considers herself a modern formalist, addressing contemporary issues in poetic verse with stylized language. <syentumi@gmail.com>

Sherry Wellborn spends a good deal of time in her garden, clipping, planting, sniffing, kneeling. She counts the winter days to February when the early bulbs emerge and the dark and cold begin to recede. Many of her journal pages are overlain with loam smudges.

Stan Zumbiel first turned his thoughts into poetry while serving in the United States Navy. In January 2008 he received his MFA in Writing from Vermont College of Fine Arts. His first poetry collection, *Standing Watch*, was published in the fall of 2016 by Random Lane Press. <Lszumbiel@att.net>

Stephen Linsteadt is a painter, poet, and writer. His recent poetry collection is titled *The Beauty of Curved Space* (Glass Lyre Press). His poetry is also published in *California Quarterly, Silver Birch Press, Synesthesia Literary Journal, Pirene's Fountain, The Poeming Pigeon,* and others. <stephenlinsteadt.com>

Steve Williams works helping people with disabilities find meaningful work. He submits to local and internet journals in order to support their efforts. He lives in NW Portland with a lovely woman who writes and edits much better than he but refuses to admit it.

Susan Rogers considers poetry a vehicle for light and positive energy. She practices Sukyo Mahikari, a spiritual practice promoting a positive lifestyle. Read her work in Best Poems of San Diego, Saint Julian's Press and elsewhere. She was nominated for a Pushcart in 2013. <saintjulianpress.com/susan-rogers.html>

Susan Whitney lives in Eugene and is lucky to have found poet friends there, especially the Red Sofa group. Sitting on the sofa with them is great fun, but listening to their poetry is the best. She will have a couple of poems published in *Verseweavers*, 2016. <whitneys@pacifier.com>

Suzanne Sigafoos is author of *Held in the Weave*. Her new book is looking for a publisher. Her poems appear in *The Oregonian; Windfall, a Journal of Poetry of Place;* and *The Knotted Bond*. Suzanne's essay, "Green." is in *Bellingham Review*, Issue 71; *VoiceCatcher* recently published her poem, "Playlist." <suzinkpdx@gmail.com>

Suzy Harris is a Portland writer who has studied with Claudia Savage. She has published in *Voicecatcher: a journal of women's voices and visions*. <suzylharris@gmail.com>

Terri Niccum enjoys watching birds take baths and horses run. Her poems have appeared in *The Poeming Pigeon: Poems About Food*; *Cadence Collective*; and *Pretty Owl Poetry*. <tniccum.com>

Tim Kahl is the author of *Possessing Yourself* (CW Books 2009), *The Century of Travel* (CW Books, 2012) and *The String of Islands* (Dink, 2015). He is also editor of *Clade Song*. He is the vice president and events coordinator of The Sacramento Poetry Center. <<www.timkahl.com>>

Tricia Knoll is a lifelong gardener who usually has dirt under her fingernails. Her poetry appears in numerous journals and anthologies. Her poetry collections include *Ocean's Laughter* (Aldrich Press, 2016); a chapbook, *Urban Wild* (Finishing Line Press, 2014); and forthcoming this summer, *Broadfork Farm* (The Poetry Box). <triciaknoll.com>

Viola Weinberg was the first Poet Laureate of Sacramento, CA. She is a Glenna Luschei Distinguished Poet, and Pushcart and Best of the Net nominated. Author of ten books of poetry, her work has been published on buses, prayer flags, tattoos and two major works of public art. <neruda@comcast.net>

W.P. Osborn's *Seven Tales and Seven Stories* won the 2013 Unboxed Books Prize in Fiction, selected by Francine Prose. His short work is in *Chicago Quarterly Review*, *Southern Humanities Review*, *Texas Review*, *Hotel Amerika*, Gettysburg Review, *Beloit Fiction Journal*, *Gargoyle*, and other journals. <wposborn.com>

Index of Poets

The following authors whose poem(s) begin on the annotated page number(s) are indexed by last name:

    Ahlen, Pamela: 90
    Angier, Heather: 21
    Averill, Diane: 70
    Avey, Dianne: 93
    Baldwin, Michael: 111
    Bloom, Irene: 108
    Brown, Katy: 38, 68
    Cadle, Lanette: 59
    Cain, Cathy: 119
    Chula, Margaret: 76
    Corrigan, Brittney: 103
    Crate, Linda M.: 64
    Creighton, Neil: 19
    Culshaw, Gareth: 56
    Davis, C. Hunter: 25
    Davis, John: 46
    Douglas Lombard, Rosemary: 65
    Eastwood, Robert: 54
    Ely, Johanna: 91
    Farr, Matt: 39
    Ferguson, Linda: 120
    Garber, Brad G.: 100
    Harris, Suzy: 24
    Hill, Ruth: 89
    Howells, Ann: 80
    Howington, Georgette: 45
    Johnston, Marilyn: 78, 99
    Kahl, Tim: 106
    Knight, Kelila A: 33
    Knoll, Tricia: 23, 95
    Kolp, Laurie: 115
    Lagier, Jennifer: 49

le Fatte, Eric: 16
LeKane-Yentumi, Shari Jo: 117
Lighthart, Annie: 118
Lind, Laurinda: 102
Linsteadt, Stephen: 82
Marriage, Alwyn: 26
Martin, Carolyn: 61, 97
McGuire, Catherine: 48
McKenzie, Carter: 67
Meier, Barbara A.: 17
Merrifield, Karla Linn: 57
Miller, Amy: 74
Morgan, Katherine: 77
Nakazawa, Liz: 87
Nash, Claudine: 85
Newberry, Emily Pittman: 50
Niccum, Terri: 32
Nicola, James B.: 37
Osborn, W.P.: 40
Palmer-Baker, Pattie: 92
Parker, Rachelle M.: 42
Pobo, Kenneth: 110
Powers, Janet M.: 94
Rinne, Cindy: 69
Roberts, Jeannie E.: 81
Rogers, Susan: 35
Russell, Scott A.: 107
Schneider, Ada Jill: 15
Schug, Larry: 47
Sigafoos, Suzanne: 60
Skillman, Judith: 52
Solomita, Alec: 101
Stoessl, Elizabeth: 73
Suter, Beth: 79
Thomas, G. Murray: 29
Thorpe, Allison: 27
Truex, Brigit: 105

Van Beek, Cheryl A.: 88
Wax, Phyllis: 83
Way, Lillo: 63
Weinberg, Viola: 116
Wellborn, Sherry: 109
Wells, Kate: 75
Whitney, Susan: 43
Williams, Daniel: 30
Williams, Steve: 113
Wilson, Sara: 44
Wright, M.: 112
Yager, Paul: 20
Zumbiel, Stan: 84

About The Poetry Box®

The Poetry Box® was founded in 2011 by Shawn Aveningo & Robert R. Sanders, who whole-heartedly believe that every day spent with the people you love, doing what you love, is a moment in life worth celebrating. It all started out as a way to help people memorialize the special milestones in their lives by melding custom poems with photographic artwork. Robert and Shawn expanded on their shared passion for creating poetry and art with the introduction of The Poetry Box® Book Publishing.

The book you now hold in your hands, *The Poeming Pigeon — A Literary Journal of Poetry,* evolved from the first issue (*Poeming Pigeons: Poems about Birds*) Each semi-annual issue will have a unique theme, with Homer, *The Poeming Pigeon* mascot, taking flight to deliver poems to poetry lovers across the globe. Details and submission guidelines can be found at www.ThePoemingPigeon.com.

As Robert and Shawn continue to celebrate the talents of their fellow artisans and writers, they now offer professional book design and publishing services to poets looking to publish their collections of poems.

Feel free to visit The Poetry Box® online bookstore, where you'll find more books including:

Keeping It Weird: Poems & Stories of Portland, Oregon

The Way a Woman Knows by Carolyn Martin

Of Course, I'm a Feminist! edited by Ellen Goldberg

Verse on the Vine: A Celebration of Community, Poetry, Art & Wine

Poeming Pigeons: Poems about Birds

The Poeming Pigeon: Poems about Food

The Poeming Pigeon: Doobie or Not Doobie?

The Poeming Pigeon: Poems about Music

Giving Ground by Lynn M. Knapp

and more ...

Order Form

Need more copies for friends and family? No problem. We've got you covered with two convenient ways to order:

1. Go to our website at www.thePoetryBox.com and click on Bookstore.

or

2. Fill out the order form. Email it to Shawn@thePoetryBox.com

Name: _____

Shipping Address: _____

_____

Phone Number: (____) _____

Email Address: _____ @ _____

Payment Method: __Cash __Check __PayPal Invoice __Credit Card

Credit Card #: _____ CCV _____

Expiration Date: _____ Signature: _____

The *Poeming Pigeon — Poems from the Garden*

# of Copies: _____

x $15.00: _____

Plus Shipping & Handling: _____
($3 per book, or $7.95 for 3 or more books)

Order Total: _____

Thank You!

Made in the USA
Columbia, SC
20 April 2017